The Nature of Adolescent Judgment

The Nature of
Adolescent Judgment

E. A. PEEL, PH.D., D.LIT.

Professor of Educational Psychology
Head of Educational Psychology Division, School of Education,
University of Birmingham

Staples Press   London

Granada Publishing Limited
First published in Great Britain 1971 by Staples Press Ltd
3 Upper James Street London W1R 4BP

ISBN 0 286 62762 0
Printed in Great Britain by
Willmer Brothers Limited, Birkenhead

Acknowledgments

I owe a lot to my Birmingham research students for testing out many of my ideas on the subject of this monograph, and to colleagues in the United States for providing much of the opportunity to complete this study of adolescent judgment.

A Fellowship at the Educational Testing Service at Princeton first enabled me to translate some of these ideas into action and my gratitude is due to Henry Chauncy, W. Turnbull and their senior colleagues.

Then through the interest of Lee Cronbach and Ralph Tyler I held a Fellowship at the Center for Advanced Study in the Behavioural Sciences at Stanford on funds provided by the Social Sciences Research Council. I was permitted to split the fellowship in order to return to Birmingham for university matters. During this period my research students and I conducted a substantial number of experimental studies. I then spent the second half of my Fellowship at the Stanford Center in completing this monograph and I thank Meredith Wilson for this opportunity. I want also to thank Dorothy Brothers for her help in preparing the draft of the material.

Thus I am indebted to those who made those visits to the United States possible and to the many opportunities for discussion with American and European colleagues working in psychology and education, who by virtue of their number must remain anonymous.

Finally, although I acknowledge gratefully the help of colleagues and students, I would not want them to be identified with any of the shortcomings of this book. These are mine.

Contents

Preface

Making judgments is a dominant feature of adolescent intellectual life. The substantive part of the book is concerned with the elaboration of a theory about the psychological nature and development of judgment and with attempts to materialise this theory by devising measures to investigate the conditions under which adolescents make judgments.

In Chapter 1, I give my views on the importance of adolescent understanding and judgment, and in Chapter 2, I outline a scheme for categorising and analysing judgments and describe material which seems capable of assessing them within this scheme. I am sure such material can be further refined and improved.

Next, by using the measuring instrument, I study the factors entering into judgment. Most important are those stemming from the judger himself—his age, ability, background, language and interests—then there is the influence of the material used, whether it is educational or social, how far it is informative, and what form the questions take. In Chapter 4, I break down the complete act of making a judgment into noticeable features: the arousal of interest and imagining, formulating and selecting of explanations, and the importance of deductive processes. This analysis is supported by reference to several experimental investigations.

Many problems in our material and social environment involve the reconciliation of opposing forms and interests in states of more or less stable equilibrium. In Chapter 5, on the fundamental importance of insight into the conditions of stability and change, I raise problems which I think will be capable of empirical investigation in the future.

The possibility of promoting mature judgment by tuition is one which must be faced by the educationalist. Chapter 6 describes experiments designed to discover how far such promotion is possible.

Concepts are the coinage of explanation and although this is assumed in the main body of the text, I thought it necessary to add a peripheral chapter on concept formation during adolescence. It is not exhaustive, but touches on important features, some of which need further investigation.

Readers experienced in problems of thinking will see that the logical, linguistic and semantic elements of judgment may have to be teased out more thoroughly, although the research described in the last section of Chapter 3 provides a starting off point.

Lastly, I comment on the adolescent intellect. Given the present modes of secondary and high school education with substantial dependence of the many of the intellectual authority of the one, then apparently we cannot expect the extensive emergence of mature judgment until mid and late adolescence. The great unponderable is whether greater opportunity for early adolescent to discuss and evaluate problems with his peers and teachers could lead to an earlier development of intellectual maturity.

CHAPTER ONE

Intellectual Development During Adolescence

i ADOLESCENT AND YOUNG ADULT THINKING

I begin with an assertion. Above all else the adolescent and young adult apprehend the inconsistencies between the actual and the possible. They are impelled to the opinion and action which characterizes their lives by a drive to reconcile this actuality of their existence with the possibilities they themselves envisage. Usually they strive to modify the actual. This going forward and outward to conceive of possibilities beyond the limits of their environment is the central feature of their intellectual life.

Such forward and outward directed thought is part of growing up to take on adult life and the irreconcilability of some of the

13

actual and the possible leads to the conflict which is so often a feature of the relations between the new generation and the old.

This overall view of adolescent thinking is not novel, for several like it are implied in the writings of educationalists and government committees on secondary and high school education. The conception was first clearly stated in Chapter 18 of Inhelder and Piaget (1958) as a final general speculation on the growth of thinking where they examined it briefly in relation to their theory of cognitive growth.

What has been lacking however is empirical study of the functioning and growth of this feature of adolescent thought. My purpose therefore is to examine more fully the intellectual processes in this capacity to evoke possibilities and set them alongside actualities.

Some comment on the problem of adolescent thinking has already been made (Peel, June 1965) and ideas introduced about the act of explaining and ways of investigating it (Peel, Chapter 10, in Lunzer and Morris, 1968). The present monograph extends the theoretical and practical examination of the nature of adolescent judging by introducing fresh results, particularly on the conditions making for the emergence of more mature judgment.

ii THE CONTEXT OF THE PRESENT STUDY

So far as I know the techniques to be described have not been tried before and some of the thinking about the problem of adolescent judgment will also be new, but at a fundamental level this study derives most from the work of Inhelder and Piaget on the growth of logical thinking, particularly that in the older children they studied. Whereas, however, they used practical science situations, here we shall construct *verbal* situations for testing out the maturity of judgment.

The subsequent analysis of the complete act of judgment will be seen to be cognate with the investigations of Duncker on problem solving and more recently with the ideas of Guilford (1956) on divergent and evaluative thinking. More marginally the study may complement, in its different topics, the work of Suchman on inquiry training, Crutchfield on generalized problem solving skills, Ausubel on higher-level learning, Bruner on thinking and educative processes and Berlyne on idea-curiosity. It has also some contact with various views on concept formation and the diffuse boundary between thought and language.

iii THE SCHEME OF ANALYSIS

The assertion that a growing awareness of possibilities marks the intellectual growth of the adolescent needs elaboration if it is to serve either as a psychological theory or for purpose of empirical testing.

By possibilities I mean ideas, theories, hypotheses, opinions, values, concepts, causes and analogies and comparisons with previous experiences. The actualities which may have to be resolved in terms of these possibilities are here-and-now events and phenomena experienced by the individual. As an *intellectual* exercise, the reconciliation of the possible and actual may therefore take more than one form.

First we may have *understanding* of the here-and-now by which we refer it to our prior and independent experiences. Understanding may reveal itself at different levels (see next Section) and it is communicated to others by the act of explaining. So a pupil understands a chemical reaction if he can relate the happenings in the test-tube to his knowledge of chemical theory. He understands the progress of the American War of Independence when he can relate its outcome to its causal factors. Other situations calling for the intellectual resolution of possibilities and actualities are more open in that several explanations may be possible. Here the thinker may have to select, by a process of *judgment*. The study of history, geography, literature, ecology and human affairs abounds with such problems. As in the case of understanding we are able to assess a person's judgments by his explanations of them. Explanation then constitutes an operational act by which understanding and judging can be assessed. What is non-explanation? Casual observations of individuals in thinking and learning situations show that it is not just nothing at all, but rather mere description of the event. When a thinker has no preconceived ideas or opinions available he cannot progress beyond straight description.

By description I mean the account of the features of an event or phenomenon without reference to previous ideas or causes. So a pupil might describe the movement of liquids we call convection without being able to explain it. In other test situations we shall see (Chapter 2) that describer-thinking may be revealed in content dominated and circumstantial responses. In between there may be varying degrees of partial explanation and it is helpful to think of the measure of understanding as a scale with merest description at one extreme and fullest explanation at the other.

The main task in this monograph then is to investigate the understanding and judgment of adolescents by calling for explanations which may be set on a description-explanation scale. We want to find out when and under what conditions adequate explanations are forthcoming during adolesence and early adulthood.

Linked with this objective will be an account of the complete act of judgment, supported by experimental material showing how it appears during adolescence. Then we consider attempts to promote understanding and judgment by instructional methods.

Mature judgment about problems concerning our environment, whether in the material, biological or social sense, nearly always involve a grasp of certain fundamental concepts of stability and change. Thus if we put a question about plant ecology or human relations, the answers have to show a sensitivity not only to the factors making for biological and social equilibria and change but also to the dynamics of their combination and co-ordination. Such concepts may be called *modal* since they determine a way of looking at the environment and form the basis on which the more *substantive* concepts of particular areas of knowledge are based. Awareness of the conditions of stability and change develops most strongly during adolescence. They merit therefore separate discussion in a study of adolescent thinking.

This text is not in the main concerned with the growth of concept formation but, since much of the act of judgment consists of referring the here-and-now to previously formed concepts, subordinate sections will be devoted to adolescent concept formation.

Summing up, our first purpose is to investigate adolescents' judgment by examining the quality of their explanations; then we consider factors entering into the judging situation. Next we examine components of the act of judging and the extent to which they appear in adolescence and finally we discuss the improvement of judgment by tuition. A discussion of concept formation is ancillary to these main aims.

iv UNDERSTANDING

Understanding is a much criticized but, in spite of that, often used word. As pointed out by Beberman (1964):

The word 'understand' and its close relative 'meaningful' have been bandied about in educational circles to a point where just about everyone pledges allegiance to the goal of teaching meaningful and understandable mathematics.

We could not, however, witness any five minutes of teaching in any subject which did not invoke the words 'understand' or 'understanding'.

Its meanings range widely and at least four appear to be significant in the present study. First consider the situation in an elementary practical science lesson where the pupils require details on how to carry out the experiment. After the procedure has been drawn up the teacher checks by asking the question: Do you understand what you have to do? Here understanding means that the thinker can translate the *words* of the instructions into *action*. This is at the level of understanding *how* to start a car or change its wheel and the problem is merely that of relating communication with doing.

Next consider a passage in a history text, describing, say, the events between Parliament and Charles I leading up to the Civil War or those preceding the American War of Independence (Schlesinger, 1969). Such material sets out essentially a pattern of *cause-and-effect* relations of varying degrees of multiplicity and proximity and of both long- and short-term influence. When the question: Do you understand? is put, it usually means: Can you follow the sequence and pattern of causes and effects? Can you follow the argument? Here there is no question of turning the words into action, but the learner has to envisage action and relate them to their consequences. The historian is also concerned with the intentions of the agents and hence the act of understanding involves evaluation of consequences in relation to intentions. The main ingredients in understanding history, current affairs and literature are a grasp of cause and effect, an ability to follow a sustained argument and a power to evaluate.

Then we may take the case of understanding science material and problems, such as the working of a siphon, the progress of a chemical reaction, or the conditions necessary to put a satellite into orbit. Such understanding entails a reference of the specific elements of each particular problem to more general concepts and laws already established independently of the situations immediately before the thinker.

Lastly there is mathematical understanding which implies, first, insight into the formal properties of such acts as counting, measuring, tying knots and loops, etc., and then the ability to follow deductive lines of thought.

These forms do not exhaust all we imply in the word understanding. There is, for example, aesthetic understanding, which lies beyond the scope of this discussion, but the last three are central to the main theme of the research to be described later. These involve *understanding a reasoned discourse in terms of cause-and-effect relations, seeing a problem in terms of higher-level concepts, sensitivity to formal relations and a capacity to follow deductive argument.*

V JUDGING

Understanding is not enough. The ultimate measure of education is its power to bring about more effective thinking and action. Only few of the situations we face in adult life are black and white and so capable of decision without conflict. Usually we face possible alternatives, as in making personal or political judgments, none of which is unambiguously better than the others. We need judgment and also the readiness to act on that judgment.

Judging is the effective decision by which we select the courses of action. We make this decision, or should do so, if the situation permits, according to the criteria it meets. We often have to throw over some advantages to gain others. The criteria of judging should be explicit to us. There may also be better modes of teaching such judgments.

Very often a judgment is made without the criteria being obvious to the thinker, who may also not be immediately aware of his way of reaching the decision. This may be what people mean by intuition. Some intuitions come off—but when they do so they are usually made by experts. A lot of the less effective intuition, snap decisions and jumping to conclusions, which mark the judgments of the less mature and less expert, are not successful. My contention is that an analysis of the mechanism of judging and a subsequent laying before the thinker of the criteria and methods involved may improve his judgments.

I propose to define judging, in relation to thinking, in the following way. Judging is a form of thinking and is therefore invoked whenever we are in a situation for which we have no ready-made answer learned off pat. But in addition, judgment refers to a situation for which there is no single final correct response to be discovered, but rather a spectrum of responses satisfying different numbers of different criteria. Some decisions, therefore, may be better than others—on certain grounds—but in extreme conditions none is outstanding and the decision turns on what the judger wants to fulfil.

The difference between thinking and judging is that between solving a simple equation and in trying to answer such questions as: *Should the expense on space research be curtailed?*, *How free should writers and dramatists be to portray violence?*, *Can pornography be justified?*, *Shall I accept this job?*, *Is it preferable now to change to dairy farming?*

Finally a brief word about education. We hear much talk of improving its intellectual quality. This is equivalent to insisting that its curricula lead to more penetrative understanding and more effective judgment and action. We are thus involved in intellectual standards of thought and action, and what we expect of pupils and students not only affects what they learn but also demands an improvement in how they think about it.

The consequent need for a study of cognitive processes to complement the thinking about curricula merely in terms of their factual and conceptual content is reflected in the writing of several authorities in education (Stanley, 1965; Bruner, 1960; Bloom, 1956; Chapter VI in Herrick and Tyler, 1950; Bower & Hollister, 1967). The Schools Council speaks of helping pupils to enter the world of ideas, to use powers of reason, and to acquire the beginning of mature judgment and of abstract ideas.

But none of these authorities is primarily concerned with the psychological and logical investigation of the nature of understanding and judgment and the only recent research referring explicitly to judgment (Abercrombie, 1960) deals with processes of perception and reasoning and substantially ends where I propose to begin.

Apart from a few relatively recent studies (Inhelder and Piaget 1958, Peel, 1962), there have been few systematic investigations into the growth of thinking during adolescence, despite the fact that learning during the secondary and high school years is most important and formative for real understanding in the upper school and higher education.

vi WHAT A STUDY OF ADOLESCENT JUDGING INVOLVES

a Empirical Instances

Almost every problem-solving situation in secondary-high school education illustrates what is evolved in an attempt to investigate adolescent judgments.

One element is the later adolescent's increasing power to use deductive reasoning and the decreasing need to draw upon induction in problems capable in some degree of solution by either method. We shall discuss later how this comes about but here is a problem which brings the differences out very clearly:

> In a knock-out championship like the Wimbledon Tennis Championship, assuming no drawn games, how many games must be played if there are 64, 30, 47 teams? Is there a general rule? Can you prove it?

When this problem was given to some 16–17 year old sixth-form pupils, only one in four could proceed beyond the inductive analysis to *prove* the general case deductively by starting from the essential structure of the problem, contained in the fact that there can be only one final winner and that each losing team is immediately eliminated (Law, 1968).

To take another field, if the understanding of liquid convection by a class of 14–15 year olds is tested by demonstrating it with laboratory apparatus or with a model domestic hot water system, most pupils will be able to describe it and make predictions relating to other applications and also to generalize the law to air convection. But very few will be able to explain the phenomena in terms of volume, expansion, density differences and gravity. Usually if an explanation is forthcoming, it puts the cart before the horse as follows: the hot water rises and the cold water comes down to take its place.

One question is whether the difference between merely describing and giving a comprehensive explanation represents a change in quality of thought. The question is necessary since one cause of the difference may be merely that of the availability of knowledge outside the phenomenon being studied; in the above case, for example, a knowledge of the concepts of density, gravity, buoyancy, etc. It may be argued that this is all there is to the difference, but there is convincing evidence to the contrary (Inhelder and Piaget, 1958). What constitutes the change in the quality of thinking — over and above the capacity to form and utilize more powerful concepts — will be developed later and supported by experimental evidence. Quality of thought is really concerned with the mental operations by which concepts are utilized.

It is not only in mathematics and science that change in quality of thinking can be seen during adolescence. It is revealed, for instance, very clearly in history and geography.

An aerial photograph of a small town built about the intersection of a road and railway in the Canadian wheat belt was shown to a group of secondary school pupils (Rhys, 1964). The picture showed as well the limitless panorama of the surrounding flat lands. Another picture accompanied it showing the harvesting of the wheat.

The pupils were then asked individually to answer the question:

Why has this small town grown up just here, where the main road and railway cross each other?

The range of answers is enlightening. The younger pupils showed little appreciation of the elements of the behavioural environment which would have guided action and no reflection upon the information presented in the picture. Thus we have:

Because the land is flat and they build houses on flat land usually. To leave all the other flat land to grow all the wheat. (Considering the fields and town and neglecting the road and railway.)

Between the ages of $12\frac{1}{2}$ and 14 the stock replies referred to the value of the railway in getting access to the wheat farms and in enabling the harvest to be transported away.

Because you can get to the wheat here by railway and road, and seeing how the railway goes straight through, it can pick up all the wheat from the farms.

> *So that the farmer can get his wheat harvest to the nearest town. The railway can carry much more than one truck and it's faster.*

The answers are dominated by the concrete pictorial evidence — the flat vastness of the wheat land and the single threads of communication going through it. There is little evidence either of *imagining* other possible factors or of making a comprehensive balanced judgment on their basis.

This quality of thought is shown in the answers of the oldest group of pupils, ages ranging from $14\frac{1}{2}$ to $15\frac{1}{2}$, where the town is seen as a focal point for the whole of the surrounding farming community. This conception includes that of the need for bulk storage, dealing with surplus harvest, services, goods and equipment for the farmer, shopping centre, etc., and the recognition of the town as a centre for inward as well as outward movement of materials, equipment, and people. Thus we have:

> *Because it is used as a central place with people bringing wheat to it to be stored and shipped off. It could be used as a central starting point and it provides a shopping centre. Also anything to be brought in for the farmer can be gathered here, and collected by the farmer later.*

These answers suggest that in thinking about geography the younger grammar and high school pupils may be well able to describe situations and sequences but show only limited capacity to offer explanations, co-ordinating several factors and involving imagined possibilities.

b Interpretation of results

The above samples of adolescent thinking in different school subjects give a hint of the variety of intellectual processes involved in making a judgment. Our problem is to find out whether we can reduce this variety to fewer basic thought processes common to most situations, to discover when they appear to be most evident, and what makes up a mature comprehensive judgment.

Several aspects of thought may be distinguished. We can analyse it, for instance, into terms of *i* its conceptual content; *ii* its operations; and *iii* the underlying logical model:

i Differences in the conceptual *content* of thought are revealed in the concreteness or abstractness of the material used and in its particularity and generality.

ii Thought processes may be described in terms of the *operations* of thinking by such adjectives as: rational, conceptual, intuitive, hypothetico-deductive, inductive, formal, focusing, convergent, divergent, descriptive, explanatory, and the like.

iii In the physical sciences, abstracted concepts are expressed or modelled in mathematical terms which can lead to consequent deductions and whose adequacy as models can be tested by the comparison of these deductions with further experiments. In psychological study we may *model* thought processes in terms of *formal logic* (of classes, relations and proposition) and test their adequacy along similar but more restricted lines. The logic of classes and relations seems to account for much of descriptive thinking while the logic of propositions well models the most mature forms of thinking seen in explanatory activity.

All three aspects of thought will be invoked in the following pages where we shall also deliberately choose empirical instances from widely different fields in order to bring out universal features of thinking.

CHAPTER TWO

Explaining and Judging

i CATEGORIZING THE JUDGMENTS

The purpose of this chapter has to do primarily with the method of investigation. In it I set out the basic theoretical framework for the research, describe the technique devised to assess the maturity of judgment of adolescents and comment on its reliability and consistency. We begin by introducing two things briefly:

Choice of test material;
Tentative categorization of the answers.

The test material consists of short anecdotes or passages commenting on some topical, social or intellectual problem about each of which a question is asked, supplemented with a second question:

Why do you think so? Each passage and its question are so devised as a unit that the first question cannot be adequately answered wholly from the content of the passage (see Section iv). In
order to produce a mature judgment the responder has to invoke
possibilities from his independent experience. This is brought out
by the second question and the answer produced by the subject
provides the necessary evidence for grading his maturity of judgment. It is assumed that the *explanation* the subject offers to the
question: Why do you think so? gives us an insight into the
quality of his judgment.

A tentative scheme for categorizing the answers was obtained
by considering the grades used in the research carried out by
Lodwick (1958; Peel, 1959), who used short passages of popular
history such as the anecdote of King Alfred and the cakes with the
question: Could Alfred cook? This brought out answers at two
clear levels; those dominated by the content of the passage and
those in which the thinker invoked possibilities not mentioned in
the passage. In younger children particularly a third level of
answer is also quite frequent, where the response shows fragmented
and inconsistent judgment.

Following upon a later research where the passages were more
precisely defined (see Section iv) three basic levels or categories
of answers were provided for:

Tautological, premise denying, partial and inconsistent
responses;
Responses based solely on selection from the given content of
the passage;
Imaginative responses in which outside ideas were invoked.

We shall see later (Section v) that it is possible to obtain more
numerous and finer categories, according to the passage material
chosen and the question asked. For instance, in Section iv we
examine test material making use of topics from agricultural geography. This regularly produced four categories of answers (see
p. 37). The third and fourth categories appear from a sub-division
of answers at the most mature level of imaginative responses into
those revealing:

a capacity to combine more than one piece of evidence with
outside ideas and to evoke cause and effect;

a more articulate invocation of explanations often implying
an awareness of the balanced nature of the geographical
environment.

ii DESCRIBING AND EXPLAINING

The distinction between content-dominated answers and imaginative responses invoking explanations is crucial in this study of
adolescent thinking. It forms the broad basis upon which the
several experiments are constructed. The transition from *content-
dominated* to *possibility-invoking* answers seemed to be the pre-
dominant feature of early and mid-adolescent thinking. Logically
restricted answers do also occur but they are associated with
younger, less able and more unsophisticated subjects. They are
more characteristic of childhood thinking—a relic remaining with
a minority of the less well-endowed adolescents.

In order to aid thought about the main distinction I draw
parallels between *a* content domination and description and *b* possibility invocation and explanation. Since the terms *description*
and *explanation* may have different shades of meaning for different
readers I propose to define and illustrate my use of the terms in
the next few pages. I distinguish between describing and explaining in a way which subsumes the meanings of understanding outlined in Chapter 1 (p. 17).

Description relates to the first definition on that list and merely
involves an account of the phenomenon and a relating of its parts
without reference to other ideas, analogies, similarities and antecedent or contiguous circumstances.

Explanation, on the other hand, entails referring the phenomenon causally to previous phenomena and independent generalizations.

Thus, a person might describe the prevailing climate of Western
Europe fairly accurately over the months, and the description would
enable one to know more or less what to expect next year. But he
has not explained the climate unless he refers to principles of
meteorology, physical geography and physics. These would include
concepts of heat transmission, convection, radiation, evaporation,
deposition, rotational spin of the earth and so on.

The following passage illustrates the difference between the simplest description, free of conceptual invocation, and explanation in the sense I am using it (Runciman, 1963).

> If, for example, an observer watches a group of people who under certain circumstances exchange small pieces of paper and metal, after which one of them gives another an object which the recipient than takes away, he may in due course be able to make accurate predictions about the transfer of goods in this community by correlating such transfers with the exchange of metal pieces. But unless he has grasped the ideas of money, buying and selling, and so on, we shall deny his claim to have explained what is going on.

In the following extract from a piece of adolescent writing:

> The earliest form of slavery in the ancient world, and that which remains the most prevalent and well known, was domestic slavery, that is slavery within the family home as against slaves engaged in mining, agriculture or manufacture. It was the earliest because the family was the basis of society in early Greece and Rome, as it was in the societies usually studied by anthropologists.

the writer is invoking the concept of family to account for the earliest known facts about slavery. This is explanation as defined in this text.

It is realistic to think of merest description and fullest explanation at the bottom and top end respectively of a scale of ascending power of explanation. Such a reservation is necessary because usually we describe in terms of language (except in the case of ostensive definition). The nouns, adjectives and verbs of language embody concepts and so it may be difficult to give pure descriptions and to avoid some element of explanation when words are used. Here is an example familiar to teachers of elementary physics:

Suppose we ask a pupil to describe what he sees in the following experiment to demonstrate convection in liquids. The glass tube loop A, B, C, D is in a vertical plane and contains water. Colouring matter is put in at A where the tube is then gently heated.

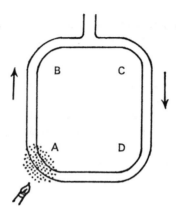

Figure 1. Experiment I

If he says the liquid *rises* from A to B, he is doing more than relating the elements of the experimental situation. He is relating happenings in the experimental situation to the wider context of terrestial geometry (rising means going away from the surface of the earth).

Description would say colour went from A to B to C to D when the liquid was heated at A.

A full explanation would refer to expansion of the liquid under heat at A, dissolving the colouring matter, displacement of the less dense warm liquid by the denser cool liquid (by gravity) and so on.

If in our response to any set of phenomena to any problem, pattern or sequence we attempt to group and relate the parts, then this is *description*, as done by younger children in Inhelder's and Piaget's cue-and-ball pendulum experiment (Chapters I and IV, 1958), in the inductive solution of the knockout competition problem mentioned in Chapter 1 or in the method of history teaching which aims to emphasize the uniqueness of the historical event. Describer-thinking answers the questions: How is this made up? What are the features?

If, however, the thinker relates the phenomena, patterns and sequences to outside concepts, wider causes and generalizations, then here we have *explanation*, as for example in relating the pendulum with gravity, in deducing the number of games in the knockout competition and in the *topic* method of teaching history.

Explainer-thinking answers the questions: Why is this so? What is its conceptual basis? What is it an instance of? In what context does it fit?

Differences between description and explanation are brought out in the following responses obtained from unpublished research (Wells, 1970) on pupils' explanation of science problems. The pupils were presented with the apparatus, no doubt known to some readers, in which a bevelled roller apparently runs *up* a widening groove (as it 'moves up' its centre of gravity is actually lowered). The pupils were asked the question: Is it true to say the roller goes uphill? Why? The following range of answers reveal different kinds and a range of quality of answers.

Table I

Inadequate description	*CA 15·1 MA 14·2	It is true that the roller goes uphill because A is ¾″ higher than B.
Sketchily descriptive	CA 12·7 MA 13·10	It is not true to say that it goes up because the middle of the roller is going down.
Fuller description	CA 14·4 MA 14·2	No. Because as it goes along the track the object is more sloped than the track and as the track gets wider the space of the roller gets more than the track and so it goes along the track uphill.
Explanations in terms of the the concept of gravity	CA 15·9 MA 19·0	It is not true to say that the roller goes uphill because unless it is powered it cannot move away from the pull of gravity.
	CA 16·8 MA 19·1	No. It is not true. Because the sides broaden to a greater extent than the one side of the roller, so the centre of gravity of the roller is going downhill.

* CA = Chronological Age.   MA = Mental Age.

iii MAKING PREDICTIONS

When a person is capable of explaining a phenomenon we usually expect him to be able to predict the outcome of similar phenomena. Thus the pupil who can explain the convection results can predict what is likely to happen in the case of a domestic hot water system. What can he predict if he is capable of giving only a mere description? The quotation from Runciman (page 27) illustrates that some prediction could follow. The power to predict future outcomes is sometimes held to be an exclusive criterion of understanding and explanation but it would seem that it does not indeed discriminate between description and explanation. What we do find however is that predictions from description are more limited. Let us look again at the simple experiment on convection.

If the pupil confined himself to the barest description A to B to C to D to A, could he predict from the experiment? Yes, in some limited cases where the whole system of circulation was in a vertical or near plane and where the source of heat was at the bottom of the system as in applications such as a domestic hot water heating system.

But how would he cope with the following?

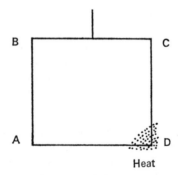

Heat

Figure 2. Experiment II

Unless he referred to 'rising' in Experiment I, he could not predict the outcome of II.

The pupil could predict the outcome in even less obvious extensions like the movement of draughts, the effect of double glazing, cavity walls, and the earth's systems of winds and air movements, only if he had invoked the much more significant concepts of expansion of fluids under heat, change in density, displacement under gravity, etc., to obtain a full explanation. The best student would have such insight that he could cope with such an apparent anomaly as the freezing of water from the top.

Simple prediction is possible from the barest description but only in situations which repeat the features of the original phenomenon. The quotation from Runciman (p. 27) implies the same thing—no doubt his observer could predict future transactions so long as the new situations embodied no more than the old, but how would his observer be able, without explanatory concepts, to predict what would happen if there were an extreme buyer's (or seller's) market, or if there were acute inflation, etc.?

iv INVESTIGATING DIFFERENCES IN THE QUALITY OF JUDGMENT

When we turn to the problem of investigating differences in the quality of adolescent explanation and judgment, our first task is to produce test material capable, at the highest level of answer, of evoking conceptual and causal thinking. Without being pretentious, we may say we want to challenge the imagination of the ablest and most mature pupils and students, so that they will look for explanations and bases of judgments beyond the actual material used. As we saw in section i, preliminary work indicated that at least three clearly marked points on this line of judgment might be kept in mind in drawing up the passage and questions. At the lowest level logically immature individuals think restrictedly and tend to answer tautologically, to be put off by irrelevances, or to deny premises or other conditions of the problem.

At the next level the thinker is dominated by the content of the material and seems unable to look outside it.

Finally, at the highest level of answer, the thinker realizes he has to go beyond the content of the passage to evoke possible hypotheses from his own experience.

I want now to illustrate the test material used by selecting three or four passages and to show the results of their application. The following passage with its questions was one devised in the first

investigation (Peel, 1966), so that the full range of responses might
be evoked:

> Only brave pilots are allowed to fly over high mountains.
> This summer a fighter pilot flying over the Alps collided with
> an aerial cable railway, and cut a main cable causing some
> cars to fall to the glacier below. Several people were killed
> and many others had to spend the night suspended above the
> glacier.
>
> (1) Was the pilot a careful airman?
>
> _____
>
> (2) Why do you think so?
>
> _____

The passage contains a leading statement which is irrelevant to the
judgment required for answering the question put to the pupil, *Only
brave pilots are allowed* ... Then follows a short section in which
a happening takes place which is related to the question, but which
by itself is not adequate or sufficient to form the basis of a judgment. The happening is *the collision with the cable.*

Thus, the question might evoke responses at least at points
where:

a irrelevancy, tautology and inconsistency may dominate
b the content (cutting the cable) solely may decide
c extenuating possibilities are invoked

Also, information might be available about the sequence inter-
mediate between points *b* and *c*. The expectation is that adolescent
thinking will mainly reveal itself in this range. The analysis of the
answers to the second question is the essential part of the investigation and it was found possible to grade the answers into four categories, as illustrated below, where *c* is the most mature.

Question:	Was the pilot a careful airman?
Answers	
Category *c*:	Yes, No, Maybe, taking account of extenua- ting possibilities, vision, weather, state of the plane
Category *bii*:	No, because if he was careful he would not have cut the cable

Category *bi* : No, because he hit the cable, etc.

Category *a* : Yes or No, with irrelevant comment or denial of the premise.

e.g. Yes, he was brave; yes, the cable shouldn't be there; no, he was a show-off

The reliability of these categorizations was measured by comparing the groupings produced independently by two judges. A product moment correlation coefficient of 0.89 (S.E. 0.005) was obtained.

The problem was given to various types of junior high and secondary school pupils (Peel, 1966). Here are the results from giving the test at New Jersey junior high and high schools. The ages of the boys and girls were as follows:

Table II Age distribution of pupils

Age	9+	10+	11+	12+	13+	14+	15+
Number	11	12	11	10	9	23	2

The results of analysing the categories of answer against chronological ages (CA) and mental ages (MA) in months were as follows:

Table III

Answer Categories	New Jersey Boys and Girls				
	CA			MA	
	n	m	s.d.*	m	s.d.*
c	24	161·2	15·5	176·2	28·8
bii	34	149·0	21·0	164·3	31·9
bi	10	145·5	21·2	140·5	21·1
a	10	124·5	17·9	134·5	23·7

* s.d. standard deviation

The existence of noticeable numbers in the categories *c*, *bi* and *a* supports the contention that the differences listed at the three points on the line of maturity appear to be brought out by the text

c

material. Furthermore, although the study is not longitudinal, the average ages associated with the different categories are suggestive. It appears that answers (Category *c*), implying thinking beyond the limited circumstantial evidence of the passage, are likely not to be frequent before ages of $13\frac{1}{2}$–$14\frac{1}{2}$. Circumstantial answers (both Categories *b*), where the content of the passage appears to dominate, even though it is only partially adequate in relation to the question, are associated with ages of 12–$13\frac{1}{2}$. The logically restricted answers (Category *a*) are not numerous. Answers in Category *bii* and Category *bi* are both circumstantial and tied by the content of the passage, but they are distinguished by an interesting logical and formal feature not foreseen in planning the research. The *bi* answers are equivalent to the direct, *modus ponens*, form of implication: If he crashed the plane, then he was not careful.

On the other hand *bii* answers are equivalent to the *modus tollens* form of implication, where a denial of the consequence leads to a denial of the antecedent: If he had been careful, he would not have crashed the plane.

Both state the same judgment but the *modus tollens* is a more sophisticated way of doing it. The age difference of some half year is to be noted. Another passage reveals an age difference of one year in this same respect.

The research was extended by devising more passages (see Appendix 1, p. 157. As examples, here are two passages with their questions and results taken from experiments described more fully later.

1 Lynn is a large town with a busy railway junction which attracts boys who are interested in train-spotting. Burton is a small place not far away and so many people who live there do their shopping in Lynn because there are more shops. British Railways have recently decided to close Burton station and run no more trains from there to Lynn.

   Q. Should Burton station be closed?
   Q. Why do you say that?

Range of answers obtained with the assessed category for each response:

   i Yes. One day a train-spotter may get killed. (*a*)
   ii Yes. The trains have stopped running. (*a*)
   iii Yes. There are lots of other railway stations. (*a*)

iv No.   The people of Burton may depend on Lynn for their
shopping. (*b*)

v Yes.   People should do their shopping in their own town
and this is good for trade. (*b*)

vi It all depends whether the people can get to Lynn any
other way (*c*)

vii It depends whether many people use the train and if they
have other ways of travelling to Lynn. (*c*)

The distribution of categories of answers among 128 secondary
school girls randomly selected in two age groups 11–12 and
13–14 + were as follows:

Table IV

| Age group | Category of Answer | | |
	Imaginative c	Circumstantial b	Restricted a
11–12	25	37	2
13–14 +	34	28	2

The relative scarcity of low-level answers is to be noted as well as
the shift from b to c responses from 11 to 13 years of age.

2 All large cities have art galleries and Italy is exceptionally
rich in art treasures. Many people travel to Italy, especially
to enjoy these old paintings, books and sculptures. Floods
in the Florence area recently damaged many of these great
works. Old paintings are rare, valuable and beautiful and
should be kept safely stored.

Q. Are the Italians to blame for the loss of the paintings
and art treasures?

Samples of answers graded as previously are as follows:

i No, not really, it's not their fault they only had to keep
them. (*a*)

ii No, because they've got lots of treasures. (*a*)

iii I don't think they are. I think it was just the weather, and
the rain had to come. (*b*)

   iv Well, I shouldn't think so, not really, because of the floods, I mean, they didn't let the flood come did they. (*b*)
   v Well, not entirely, but they were partly because they could have put them somewhere where they weren't damaged by the floods, but if there was nowhere to put them then they were not to blame. (*c*)
   vi Well, not completely, they could have been kept safe, unless the floods took them completely by surprise. I suppose they did, but it might be best to protect them in glass cages. (*c*)

The distribution of grades of answer by age was as follows:

Table V

| | Category of Answer | | |
Age group	Imaginative *c*	Circumstantial *b*	Restricted *a*
11 0–12 11	5	15	1
13 0–15 2	12	12	3

All three of the above tests appear to bring out well the general differences between a circumstantial opinion, limited by the content of the passage, and a more comprehensive, imaginative judgment enriched by the thinker. The feasibility of preparing similar tests from school material, particularly on geography and history, seemed to be assured.

   A good start on the subject of adolescent thinking in terms of school material was made by Rhys (1964). He chose the subject of agricultural geography from which to construct his test material. He stated the problem of making geographical judgments in these terms:

   Throughout this investigation I have operated from the basic premise that the understanding of geographical material at the secondary stage compels the adolescent to place a person other than himself in an environment other than his own, and furthermore, he must take into account the complex interplay of a miscellany of factors within that foreign environment.

The environment in this case being taken to mean the Behavioural Environment—a particular field of human action —involving an appreciation of human physical forces active within a particular setting.

He used several media for presenting simple geographical problems, not requiring a lot of technical knowledge. The media included a prose passage, pictures, maps, plans and demographic and other statistical tables and diagrams, which related to farming in five areas —in the Andes, the wheat belt of Canada, and Japan, the seasonal migrations of the Masai with their cattle and the socio-economic population problem of the crofters in the Hebrides.

First I select a question based on the passage about farming in the Andes. The passage was taken from a school text and is perhaps longer than necessary for the purpose of the test—but it conveys a good geographical problem setting. (See Appendix 2, p. 161.) It was concerned with soil erosion produced by cutting down trees and subsequent excessive cropping. The question asked:

Why did the deep fertile soil cover disappear and make farming impossible?

The answers could be grouped into four main categories:

Category 1 Largely tautological, repeating parts of the passage verbatim or in a slightly modified form.

Casual irrelevant guesses: 'Because the sun was so very hot.' 'Because it was a bad brook.'

Lack of understanding: 'Because there were tall trees growing on the good soil.'

Category 2 Attempted analysis in terms of the presented data. Some attempt at interpretation even if only partial and incomplete. Seizing on one piece of circumstantial evidence to support a simple unqualified inference.

Characteristic responses: 'Because the big trees had been chopped down.' 'The soil was washed away by flooding.' Simple recognition of a destructive element with no appreciation of the fact that it had not operated in the state of natural equilibrium which existed before.

Category 3 A growing capacity to combine more than one piece of evidence and a clear awareness of cause and effect.

'Because when the trees were taken away, the rain fell direct on to the soil washing it away down the hillside.'

Category 4   A more detailed and thorough examination, going beyond a comprehensive list of interlocking destructive factors to suggest that the farmer was unwise, for example, to farm in such an area or to carry out the actions he did. There is a more positive awareness of the balanced nature of a geographical environment and that when man interferes with this balance there is a general disturbance of all the interlocking forces.

'Through getting rid of the trees, he made it possible for the rain to wash the good soil away. This is so because the roots of the trees hold the soil in place. The fact that he always planted maize would not have helped when farming the crops should be changed to replace what the other crops take out.'

Rhys obtained high judge reliability (.95) between people assigning the answers to these categories and, when he calculated the mean ages (chronological and mental) of the pupil answering in each category, he found the following statistics:

Table VI   (Ages in months)

		CA		(MA Raven's Matrices Test)	
Category of answer	n	m	s.d.	m	s.d.
Restricted 1	21	135·6	10·5	138·1	17·7
Circumstantial 2	26	141·5	12·6	147·1	15·3
Comprehensive					
circumstantial 3	33	160·3	14·4	166·9	17·9
Imaginative 4	40	180·4	10·2	195·4	19·0

Again, we see clear differences in maturity of judgment by age and, as in the 'Pilot' New Jersey results, the standard deviation associated with mental age are somewhat larger.

Beginning with a fairly limited capacity to offer explanations in terms of single pieces of circumstantial evidence, the thinker is gradually able to co-ordinate several such elements in the problem situation and finally he is able to see these as elements in a system of balance which is disturbed by human action.

V GRADING THE JUDGMENTS

Two related things are important: the degree of agreement between different assessors of the judgments made by the pupils; and the number of categories possible within the grading scale.

Earlier exploratory work (Peel, 1959) showed that comprehension material was capable of evoking responses at three noticeable points and that it was necessary to telescope larger numbers of categories in order to achieve reproducability as required by Guttman's technique for discovering whether any chosen set of grades constitutes a scale. In the first main enquiry (Peel, 1966) and others that immediately followed it (Anderson, Best, Brydon, Millett, all 1967), the three basic categories of restricted, circumstantial and imaginative thinking were utilized.

Assessor reliability was measured by the degree of agreement between asssessors who had the same instructions about the 3-point scaling device and the same instances to support it. Correlation coefficients of .97 and .89 were obtained for the 'Jane' and 'Pilot' tests respectively (Peel, 1959).

Similarly high reliabilities were found by the other investigators. For example Brydon obtained assessor rehabilitation between .84 and .90 based on the answers of 96 pupils each doing six test-passage tasks. Best obtained only 72 cases of disagreement between assessors out of a total of 640 assessed responses. Anderson asked 11 assessors to grade the pupils' responses on the 3-point restricted–circumstantial–imaginative scale and obtained good agreement. An example of their grading of eight answers to the Burton railway problem is given in Appendix 3 on page 163.

As already mentioned, Rhys found it desirable to use four categories by dividing at the upper end of the scale. Over his twelve sets of response he obtained correlation coefficients ranging from .95 to .98 between the placings of the responses by independent assessors. This represents a very high degree of assessor reliability.

Some of our enquiries have suggested finer features of judging within this range. These include the growing capacity with age to consider more than one element at a time, even though the judgment is circumstantial. Other investigations bring out the structural quality of some mature thinking when the judger is aware of the interacting nature of the elements in the social, historical, geographical or science situation. But very often the subjective nature of some of these finer graduations is brought out when we examine the scaled answers by the Guttman technique. Usually a reduction to three or four categories is necessary. Stones (1967) however found it possible to utilize six categories in her study of the historical thinking of secondary school pupils. (See p. 126.)

vi CONSISTENCY OF THE PUPILS' JUDGMENTS

The question of the stability of a person's level of thinking in different situations has often been raised, particularly in connection with the assertion that there are developmental stages. In the work now being described, the issue is better seen as a question of consistency of judgment over different comprehension-test situations. We have not measured reliability of judgment by a test-retest situation but have confined ourselves to correlating performance on different passages. One reason for not using the same passage on two occasions is that there may be quite a marked learning effect.

One research (Peel, 1966, p. 86) revealed a correlation between the pupils' level of measuring the 'Pilot' and 'Jane' passages of .347 (product moment), S.E. $= .003$. This is very significant for what are indeed single-item tests, each scored on a 5-point scale.

Brydon gave six passage-tests and questions (see Appendix 1), and a calculation of the product moment correlation between the combined score on the first three passages and a similar one on the last three passages revealed a figure of .82 which certainly suggests a high degree of consistency of level of judgment across different test situations. The agreement between levels of answer, a—restricted, b—circumstantial, c—imaginative, obtained from Brydon's test items 1 and 2 is well indicated in the following covariation table.

Table VIII Frequency of answers at the three levels Pilot Problem Cigarette smoking problem

Level of answer	Restricted	Circumstantial	Imaginative
Restricted	4	3	
Circumstantial	1	16	6
Imaginative		7	11

Casual inspection of the gradings obtained by pupils in different passages used by other investigators (Anderson, Rhys and Best) suggests a similar degree of agreement between different tests.

From the above work we may conclude tentatively that if the passages do not differ greatly in difficulty, sophistication and area of coverage they will evoke answers from any one person at not too disparate levels. However there are differences (Peel, 1959) and a necessary and fruitful line of enquiry would be to ask what we mean by difficulty, technicality and abstractness of ideas, and complexity of structure and to compare levels of answer with variations in passage difficulty and area of human knowledge.

vii SUMMING UP

In this chapter we have had two major purposes in mind, to set before the reader the main theoretical framework for grading adolescent judgments and to illustrate the practical technique used for bringing out the differences in maturity of judgment.

Discussion of the principal differences between content-dominated (circumstantial) responses and judgments implying the imagination of possibilities is supplemented by a consideration of the parallel differences between describing and explaining. Subordinate to this discussion was the problem of what kinds of predictions are possible from describing and explaining.

The essence of the technique is to present short passages with questions, which cannot be answers adequately on the basis solely of information directly given in the passages. The purpose is to provide the judger with the opportunity to draw from his independent experience and ideas in order to reach an answer.

Although most of the tests are short passages of informational prose we have used pictorial material, aerial photographs, maps, diagrams, apparatus and tables of demographic statistics and also, in order to bring out logico-linguistic elements, precisely constructed passages embodying logical propositions.

The technique is designed to produce a wide range of answers which may be grouped into three basic categories as follows:

Restricted   —tautological,   premise-delaying,
                                  irrelevant

Circumstantial   —bound solely by the content of
                                    the passage, often taking account
                                    at first of only one element

Imaginative-comprehensive—Involving the invocation of in-
                                    dependent ideas and the con-
                                    sideration of the problem in
                                    their terms

These three basic categories may be subdivided into finer divisions according to the nature of the passage-question unit and the population tested. Various investigations have produced three, four, five, six and even higher numbers of grades. However there is the risk of subjectivity with larger numbers of categories.

Thought during and after adolescence reveals itself chiefly in the range of circumstantial and imaginative-comprehensive judgments.

The illustration of the practical techniques used to bring out differences in judgments included also tables of results, showing the relation of maturity of judgment against age. These revealed a meaningful trend and, coupled with the high degree of reliability between those grading the pupils' judgments, seem to indicate that the techniques were extracting a rich array of answers across the range from content-restricted to comprehensive judgments.

CHAPTER THREE

Factors Entering into Judgment

i A SUMMARY OF POSSIBLE FACTORS INFLUENCING JUDGMENT

We may group these factors conveniently under the three headings:
  Person variables;
  Passage variables;
  Question variables.

PERSON VARIABLES

Here we look at any element in the testee's psychological make-up or environmental influences, which may bear on the maturity of his judgment.

These may include: age, sex, intelligence, personality (e.g., stable-neurotic, extravert-introvert), language attainment and usage, psychological adjustment and normality, interests, attitudes and the influences of instruction and prejudice. On the environmental side we could consider socio-economic differences, and education.

PASSAGE VARIABLES

These will include subject matter: general comprehension, history, geography, science, archaeology, etc.; differences in logical, linguistic and semantic structure; differences in preparing the student for answering the questions by giving him some instruction or additional information about the problem situation set up in the test material; differences between prose, diagrammatic, pictorial, and apparatus material; differences between passages depending on a social and a non-social problem situation.

QUESTION VARIABLES

Here we are concerned mainly with the form of the question. Since a basic feature of the technique is to attempt to challenge the thinker to support his judgments from his own ideas, the mode of challenge might be significant in evoking an imaginative response.

The following forms of question have been considered:

1 Was X ... ?
   Why do you think so?
   Calling either for a written response or a spoken one in which the experimenter may probe further (see Lodwick, op. cit., Peel, 1959, op. cit.).
   A variation on the written response is to compare answers in which the subject writes as much as he wishes with those in which he is restricted to a narrow band of number of words, say 30–50, for producing an answer.

In the above circumstances the judgment is scored on the basis of the reply to the **why?** question.

   2 The thinker is challenged in a most open and direct way when he is asked: What problem do you see?
He is given no lead as in the first type of question:
Was X...?

This form may well be suited to adolescents who often respond better the more open and undirected the situation appears to be.

   3 At the other extreme we may use a multiple-choice form of question, utilizing answers obtained independently from other groups of pupils which cover the range of maturity of answers along the whole scale of *a* restricted, *b* circumstantial and *c* imaginative-comprehensive judgments.

   4 Some test material may lend itself more readily to instructions embodying Guilford's double process of divergent and evaluative thinking. In this case the passage or other material would be followed by such instructions as:
Give as many explanations (causes, etc.) as you can.
Select the best one (or the one you prefer) and justify your choice (say why).

Here both statements can be analysed and scored.

From these many possible influences upon judgment I selected the following for imediate study: age and ability, socio-economic level, language usage, amount of information in the passage, logical-semantic structure of the test material and question form.

   Usually the above variables have been studied up to four or five at a time by choosing a population divided by age, sex, or ability, etc., and assigning various passage and question treatments to randomly selected groups of pupils within each of the major population divisions.

ii PERSON VARIABLES

a Age and ability

Although we have not carried out a longitudinal study, the cross sections chosen at different ages were, so far as we could judge from the schools and populations tested, free of systematic bias due to selection or fall out of individuals. Hence the differences we demonstrate at different chronoligcal and mental ages would appear to be really linked with them.

It will be more helpful and valid to concentrate on the two higher features on the scale of judgment, that is, on the circumstantial and the explanatory modes of response—more helpful because these features and the transition between them marks much of adolescent and adult thinking—more valid because any age association with the prelogical answers is to some extent an artefact of the lower limit of age-sampling.

From the original research (Peel, 1966, pp. 80–1), it may be noted that explanatory judgments, invoking ideas, seem to be associated with chronological ages upwards of 160 months (13 years 4 months) and in the single population, where a mental age was also available, with mental ages of 176 months (14 years 8 months) upwards.

Answers categorized as being circumstantial and restricted to passage content appeared to be linked with an age range of 140 + to 160 months (12 + to 13 +) in both the chronological and the mental sense.

A later research in the project carried out by Best, (op. cit.) using

Table IX Chronological and Mental Ages for Non-Social and Social Passages
(obtained from a population of secondary modern pupils)

Ages	Category	Non-Social			Social		
		n.	mean	s. d.	n.	mean	s.d.
Chron.	circumstantial	62	13y 5m	1y 2m	94	13y 4m	1y 2m
	comprehensive-imaginative	25	14y	1y 1m	63	13y 10m	1y 2m
Mental	circumstantial	62	12y 11m	2y	94	12y 10m	2y 1m
	comprehensive-imaginative	25	15y 5m	2y 1m	63	14y 5m	2y 3m

Table X Ages associated with different levels of judgment

Test material and Question	Age in years and months	Level of judgment			
		1	2	3	4
Paragraphs on soil erosion produced by an Andean farmer	n	11	47	29	33
Why had this not happened before when there were trees in the ground?	CA	10:10	12:0	13:8	15:5
	MA(R)*	10:4	12:9	14:8	16:0
	MA(S)*	10:9	13:10	14:8	16:0
Map showing the twice-yearly migration of the Masai with their cattle in and out of the Rift valley, with explanatory notes.	n	13	35	25	47
	CA	10:11	11:8	13:2	15:0
Why do the Masai make this twice-yearly movement in accordance with the seasonal pattern shown on the map?	MA(R)	11:1	12:1	14:3	16:0
	MA(S)	12:2	13:3	14:9	15:9
Photographs of prairies and a small prairie town.	n	16	14	56	33
Why has this small town grown up just here, where the main road and railway cross each other?	CA	10:8	11:0	13:2	15:2
	MA(R)	11:1	12:1	13:9	16:4
	MA(S)	11:11	13:6	14:3	16:1
Detailed plan of a Japanese village and a photograph and a brief prose commentary.	n	9	42	30	39
	CA	10:6	11:11	13:6	15:0
Why do you think the Japanese farmer lives in the village with his land scattered in a number of places?	MA(R)	10:8	12:4	14:2	16:1
	MA(S)	13:9	13:6	14:5	15:5

Table X—continued

Demographic charts, maps of the land and statistics showing agricultural activities of crofters.	n	13	31	37	9
	CA	10:7	11:10	13:3	15:2
Are the crofters making sensible use of their land by growing only a few crops in a small area?	MA(R)	10:11	12:8	14:1	16:3
	MA(S)	11:10	13:3	14:7	16:0

R   Ravens Matrices   S   Simplex

more passages of a similar kind to and including both the original passages, substantially confirmed these ages associated with the circumstantial and imaginative responses. (Table IX).

Other research material discussed later brings out the significance of the years 13 and 14 in the appearance of a noticeable number of imaginative judgments.

For the study of school material we may well look at the chronological and mental ages found by Rhys to be associated with the different levels of judgment described on p. 37, Chapter 2. Here is an analysis of the answers to five questions, one on each of the five sets of geographical problem material. (Table X).

If we take level 3 judgments, at the comprehensive circumstantial level, as representing the beginnings of mature judgments we notice that they do not appear with marked frequency until 13+ of chronological age and 14+ of mental age, while established mature judgment at the imaginative level 4 is associated with a chronological age of 15 and mental age of 16. The narrowly content-confined circumstantial judgments seem to be characteristic of 12 year olds, while the relatively few prelogical restricted responses are made by the youngest group. I use the term prelogical in a purely educational sense since such judgments are educationally confusing and lead to no further progress. However, logically and psychologically they are better described as being merely restricted, for they are at the beginning of a continuous albeit irregular development sequence.

b Socio-economic level of the home and the pupil's quality of judgment

It had been demonstrated in an early preliminary use of the 'Jane' passage as an English comprehensive test in an 11+ examination that children coming from intellectually superior homes tended to judge significantly better than children from less advantageous homes. This difference appeared to be quite marked even when the two groups of pupils were matched for verbal reasoning ability, as measured by the customary verbal tests.

In order to check this preliminary finding, Brydon included socio-economic level as one of the variables in his study of the effects upon adolescents' judgment of age, sex, intelligence, amount of background information provided in the passage, and socio-economic status of the parents.

Using the Registrar-General's classification he was able to group his population of 96 secondary school pupils into 5 socio-economic groups, group 1 being the highest and group 5 the lowest, and in the following table they are accompanied by their mean I.Q.s.

Table XI Distribution of children in the five social classes and their mean IQs

Social Class	5	4	3	2	1
No. of children	1	34	36	23	2
Mean I.Q.s	81	100·4	103·3	113·6	112·0

The numbers in each group are unequal owing to random selection of the sample.

The answers to the questions set on the six passage test were scored numerically on the three-point scale, and when all six scores for all children were correlated with the socio-economic level of their parents a product moment coefficient of .283 was obtained (n=96 x 6=576). The actual co-distribution of judgments was as follows:

D

Table XII Level of judgment

		restricted	circumstantial	imaginative
(high)	1	2	5	5
Socio-	2	2	52	83
economic	3	18	134	64
class	4	34	113	58
(low)	5	3	3	

From this material it would appear that maturity of judgment i
the situations used in these investigations is associated with th
socio-economic level of the home. The preliminary investigatio
carried out in the 11 + examination has significance here, for in
there are two private preparatory schools drawing exclusively upo
the sons of the upper and professional classes. In such homes idea
tend to be discussed and language may be used for purposes o
rational discussion in a much more prevalent way than in many
working class homes. There is of course also the possibility that th
differences are in part due to differences in intellectual capacity a
the third line of Table XI suggests.

c Language usage

We may therefore examine two sources for a possible link betweer
maturity of judgment and socio-economic level: innate intellectua
capacity and language usage. The influence of the former has beer
demonstrated in section iia. As to the latter we need tried tests o
the use of language. Lawton (1969) has produced such materia
depending exclusively on grammatical and lexical categories. Ar
earlier research worker, Flesch (1950), devised a scheme for analys
ing a person's written work in terms of the 'definiteness' of the
description and ideas produced. He then inverted the 'definiteness'
to give a measure of abstraction revealed in the writing. This latte
analysis is perhaps more significant than Lawton's when we think
of maturity of judgment, for it is an attempt to analyse the thinking
used whereas Lawton is primarily concerned with the language.
However since maturity of judgment, as we have defined it, may
depend on language capacity as well as ability to generalize and

bstract we have used both methods in a preliminary comparison
etween productive writing and maturity of judgment (Bartholo-
new, 1970). We obtained a measure of maturity of judgment by
iving each pupil several passage problems and then gave him the
awton material on sentence completion and free writing. We
nalysed this free writing also by the Flesch scheme.

Comparison between maturity of judgment and elements in the
awton analysis revealed marginal positive association between
udgment and the use of subordinate clauses and slightly negative
ssociation (as would be expected) between judgment and the
imple co-ordinations involving the word *and*. There was also overall
a slight association between maturity of judgment and the use of
ncommon words. Finally there was a clear positive association
with the use of the impersonal pronouns as subjects of sentences
and a negative association with the use of personal pronouns. Both
trends would be expected.

Turning to the analysis of the writing in terms of the scheme
suggested by Flesch we found a significant negative association
between the number of 'definite' words and maturity of judgment.
For instance the twenty most mature judgers had a mean Flesch
'definiteness' score of 30.1, whereas the twenty least mature judgers
scored 38.5. The difference of 8.4 is statistically highly significant.
This we would expect according to the nature of mature judgment
of the passages and the words classified by Flesch as 'definite'
which on the whole tended to be concrete and particular.

The research so far carried out has been of a preliminary nature
but it suggests promising leads for more extensive investigations.

iii PASSAGE VARIABLES

a The amount of background information provided in the passages

A question which came to mind early in these investigations of
adolescent judgment was whether the essential element is merely
the availability of knowledge and independently formed concepts,
or whether there is something more inherent in the thinker, like a
readiness to use information, which is likely to appear when a
certain intellectual maturity has been reached.

It is not an easy question to attempt to answer on experimental
evidence, but one way might be to proceed as follows. Two passages are prepared in relation to a single question, the second
having an added paragraph giving more information. This additional information would be such that if a person, answering at
the mature imaginative c level on the first passage, were responding solely on the basis of availability of information, he would tend
to give the same answer to the second passage, but now in virtue
of the additional passage information at the circumstantial b level.
If, however, the thinker was really impelled by an urge to fit the
problem into his cognitive structure he would seek to explain it
and to invoke further thinking in order to account for it and
would produce on the second occasion a different answer involving
new ideas and therefore scored at the imaginative c level.

If this latter were the case we could conclude that judgment is
more than responding to available information and that it involves
an urge to resolve the problem in terms of the thinker's cognitive
processes, one of which would be the readiness to conjure up
further ideas and possibilities.

For example the problem of the 'Florence flood' was both given
in its simple form described in the last chapter and also with an
added paragraph so that the whole passage read:

All large cities have art galleries and Italy is exceptionally
rich in art treasures. Many people travel to Italy, especially to
enjoy these old paintings, books and sculptures. Floods in the
Florence area have recently damaged many of these great
works. Old paintings are rare, valuable and beautiful and
should be kept safely stored.

The authorities knew the river was going to flood within the
next day, and the Florentines knew that many of their
churches, museums and art galleries stood below flood water
level.

The same question was asked on each occasion:
Are the Italians to blame for the loss of the paintings and art
treasures?

The same three-point method of grading the answers was used as
for the passage without the added paragraph. Examples of answers
at the three levels to this extended passage are as follows:

Level a—restricted

Not completely, because they knew it was going to flood but they didn't know exactly when.

No, because the river burst the banks.

Level b—circumstantial

Yes, because if they knew there was going to be a flood next day they should have got their paintings and everything out and taken them elsewhere.

Yes, they should have put them somewhere else to save them when they found out the river was liable to flood.

Yes, because they knew the river was going to flood and knew they would lose them.

Level c—imaginative

Well perhaps the warning came too late to get them out because they would have to be very careful to get them out and if they had had time to send the specialists out they might have—I think they could have helped a lot by blocking the churches up.

Well yes and no, they should have tried to get the more costly ones to higher ground and those that were less costly they should have left till last.

Well they are to blame in one way because they had a day's warning and they could have got some of them away if not all of them, but then they're not to blame in another way because well, they've got, or had the people to think about and I think the people are more valuable. They ought to lose the paintings before the people.

The level c answers illustrate what is happening when the added information is given. They suggest that the thinker may be provided with a deeper insight into the problem and that in those thinkers possessing the mature mechanism of thought (see Chapters 4 and 5, fresh ideas are evoked. But, if these mechanisms are not sufficiently developed, then the deeper insight is also lacking.

Brydon prepared in this way a second form of each of his passages and used the principles just described for the answers. He obtained the following frequency distributions of answers at the three levels a, b, c from the four groups of pupils tested, boys and girls responding to passages with and without added information.

Table XIII Frequencies of responses in the three categories of answers given by boys and girls under two alternative conditions concerning the amount of information provided in the passages.

	Boys		Girls	
Answers	Without added information	With added information	Without added information	With added information
imaginative	55	51	53	46
circumstantial	81	75	65	87
restricted	8	14	26	11

When these grades were scored, 1, 2, 3, beginning with restricted responses, there were no significant differences between the means and standard deviations with and without added information for each of the two groups of boys and girls.

In another research (Hilton, 1968) passages were analysed for the number of pieces of information and acts of judgment that each contained in relation to the questions asked on it, after being chosen so that six contained many and six contained few such pieces and judgments. They were then all given with their questions to the same groups of 12, 13, 14 and 15 year olds, whose answers were then analysed for evidence of new information and judgments. These were then compared with the use of information and judgments already contained in the passages.

Table XIV Number of pieces used or invoked in the answers

	6 passages containing fewer		6 passages containing more	
	used from passages	new material	used from passages	new material
Pieces of information	554	731	1000	788
Acts of judgment	30	1007	322	1103

Overall the condition of more information and judgments in the passages produced a slightly *greater* number of new pieces of information and fresh acts of judgment. Table XIV shows the totals for the entire population tested.

It seems that providing extra information in the passage sets off further processes of invoking facts and ideas and apparently the readiness hypothesis is confirmed.

b Social and non-social passages

The first investigation (Peel, 1966) revealed that the 'Jane' passage, involving a girl in a domestic problem, was more maturely answered by girls than by boys. This suggested the wider hypothesis that social problems might be more readily solved at a mature level than non-social material. In one investigation six social and four non-social passages were constructed (Best, 1967). The social passages referred to problems directly experienced and thought about by adolescents and young adults and the non-social passages were either knowledge-orientated or drew on more remote problem situations.

Here is a passage with a social content, together with the alternate forms of questions (see Section iva) asked about it.

There is always something interesting happening at a Youth Club and plenty of people go. One night there were six people there.

Why question: 'Why were there that number there that night?'
What question: 'What problem do you see here?'

Examples of the range of answers obtained are as follows:

		Grade of answer
(Why)	Because it was interesting	restricted
(What)	There was fun there. There's games and snooker and they have records on and it's somewhere to go on the nights.	restricted
(What)	Well it says there's always something happening there and yet it says there's only six people there. I think the problem of this is even though there	circumstantial

is only six people there they say it's interesting. I think the problem of this is that there's not enough people to go to really make it as interesting as it could be as a Youth Club.

(What)   I don't see any problem because it   circumstantial might have only been a small Youth Club in the middle of a village or something. I mean a Youth Club I went to it only had about fourteen members.

(Why)   There was perhaps something more   imaginative interesting on the television or there could have been a dance or there could have been someone there who the people didn't like.

Sixty-four secondary school boys and girls, 32 of each, of average and less-than-average ability answered all the ten passages. The distribution of their answers in the three grades of restricted, circumstantial and imaginative categories was as follows:

Table XV Boys' and Girls' Responses to Social & Non-social Passages

	Restricted	Circumstantial	Imaginative	Total
All responses	268	234	138	640
Boys	135	119	66	320
Girls	133	115	72	320
Responses to 6 social passages	137	146	101	384
Responses to 4 non-social passages	131	88	37	256
% responses to social	35·7	38·0	26·3	
% responses to non-social	51·2	34·4	14·4	

From this table it may be seen that while there is no difference between the overall response of boys and girls there are clear differences between the responses to social and non-social material, the former being more mature. A similar trend is revealed in Table IX on page 46.

It seems that situations which are familiar to adolescents will arouse more considered and imaginative judgments.

iv QUESTION VARIABLES

a Why...and What...form of question

As suggested in the opening paragraph of this book, adolescent thought seems to be characterized by the capacity to invoke ideas and to see problems in a way specific to adolescents. It may be possible to test this potentiality by using a very open form of question in the passage problems. The same material was given with the alternate forms of question:

1 Was X ... ? Why do you think so?

2 What problem do you see here?

The first form of question is the customary one we have used and the second gives the thinker more complete freedom of judgment. Best made these alternative question forms one of the variables in his investigation (1967) and a few answers to the open form of question are given in the last section. He found that this open form produced the same range of answers, restricted, circumstantial, imaginative, but that the situation was more difficult in that fewer mature and more immature answers were obtained. The distribution of answers to the two question forms was as follows.

Table XVI

Question form	Restricted	Circumstantial	Imaginative	Total
Why ... ?	76	156	88	320
What ... ?	192	78	50	320

When the answer levels were scored 1, 2, 3 respectively beginning with restricted answers as 1, analysis of variance show a contribu-

tion from different question forms at the one per cent level. There
is then a significant difference in the level of response to the two
question forms, but we must recall that this population was made
up of pupils of average and less-than-average intellectual ability.
A preliminary investigation with abler pupils suggested that the
shift may not be so marked in these circumstances.

b **Multiple-choice form of answer**

The effect of using a multiple-choice form of answer as opposed
to the customary form of question – Was X ... ? Why do you think
so? – has also been studied (Anderson, 1967). The alternatives in
the 5-fold multiple choice include responses at all three main levels
of restricted, circumstantial and imaginative responses. We took
these responses from those obtained in a preliminary try out. The
difference between the two forms may be exemplified from the
railway problem outlined in Chapter 2, page 34.

   1 Customary form
     Should Burton station be closed? Why do you think so?
   3 Multiple choice form
     Should Burton station be closed?
   i It should be closed because the people would then have to
     do their shopping in their own town and this would be good
     for trade.
  ii It should be closed because the trains have stopped running.
 iii It depends on how many people use the trains and whether
     they have other ways of travelling.
  iv It should be closed because one day one of those boys spot-
     ting trains is likely to fall off the platform in front of a
     train and get killed.
   v It should not be closed because the people of Burton will
     not be able to do their shopping and the shops will not have
     much trade.

Among his variables Anderson studied the influence of these question forms and of instruction in thinking. The frequency of mature
imaginative judgments obtained from 128 secondary school girls

arranged in cells according to the question and instruction conditions are set out below.

Table XVII Frequency of imaginative responses
(Maximum possible in each cell is 256)

	Not instructed	Instructed
Multiple Choice form	165	195
Why ?	70	164

The effect of the multiple-choice form of answering is clearly brought out, particularly since it is related to the effect of a short course of independent instruction on how to think (see Chapter 6). The multiple choice acts itself as a teaching aid.

V LOGICAL, LINGUISTIC AND SEMANTIC ELEMENTS

The material so far described has been designed with the primary aim of producing a wide array of answers across the range from circumstantial, content-restricted responses to comprehensive, imaginative judgments. At certain points finer logical features have appeared as in the use of the alternative but equivalent forms of argument of implication:

i An assertion of the premise leading to an assertion of the consequence.

ii A denial of the consequence leading to a denial of the premise.

We now turn to the possibility of designing passages and questions which predominantly bring out logical and linguistic elements although the semantic features associated with circumstantial and imaginative answers will also be present. Such passages in relation to the questions asked upon them still have to have an 'open' element, but this and the rest of the material is strictly tailored to certain logical forms, involving binary propositions.

We are enabled to ask such questions as: How far does the

thinker follow strictly what is given? How far does he *assume*
logical conjunctions not actually given? How far does he extend
association or contiguity of events to cause-and-effect relationship?

One such passage and question (Peel in Lunzer and Morris,
1968, p. 315) tests the reaction of the thinker to an act which is a
conjunction of two actions, moving and wearing skates. Here it is:

> *i* I've seen Mary standing at the edge of the skating rink with
> skates on her feet. I often see her walking and running to
> school and standing about. I've seen her watching the skat-
> ing at the rink and she is always talking about skating.
>
> 1 Can Mary Skate?
> 2 Why do you think so?

In the passage we have three binary conjunctions given, but *not*
the fourth, the conjunction of moving on skates which is essential
to skating.

The oldest and the ablest few pupils apparently read the passage
rigorously but feel that all has not been told and so leave the
answer open. When we turn to the 'No' answers which follow the
sentences strictly and logically, we see that abler and older pupils
tend to need to elaborate or offer explanations, justifications or ex-
tenuations. The 'Yes' answers tend to come from younger and less
able pupils.

Thus, even when they recognize the logical limitations of the
passage in relation to the question asked, the abler and more mature
thinkers reveal a certain need to fill in the gaps by evoking fresh
ideas to explain the events.

The following problem, based on the binary proposition of
implication has also yielded interesting results:

> I was looking at my friend's rose garden. He had been spray-
> ing his rose leaves with a chemical to kill a leaf disease. I saw
> sprayed leaves which were healthy and I saw unsprayed leaves,
> some of which were diseased and some healthy.
>
> 1 Can I say anything definite about the effect of the spray on
> the disease?
> 2 Why do you think so?

We can look upon this as a problem either in propositional logic
or in the multiplication of classes.

According to the first we have the propositions *the leaves are sprayed*, s and *the leaves are healthy*, h. The passage is based on the conjunctions sh, $\bar{s}h$, and $\overline{sh}$ but no reference to the absence of sprayed diseased leaves, that is the excluded conjunction, $s\bar{h}$. The passage therefore does not give a full statement of *implication*.*

The question leads the pupil to think of the implication $s \supset h$ and the analysis of his reply to the questions shows how far and in what circumstances and upon what basis he makes his judgment.

Postgraduate students and pupils from high and junior high schools were tested.

The answers to the second question: Why do you think so? — provide the main source of information. The answers were analysed with the following questions in mind:

How many subjects would read the problem in a strictly logical manner?

Would the pupils assume that all sprayed leaves were healthy?

What actual binary propositions or combined classses would be used to support this conclusion?

How far would a subject assume the spray would be effective and then concentrate upon explaining the particulars of the actual anecdote (the act of spraying or the occurrence of healthy and diseased leaves)?

It was possible to categorize the answers into five groups

   i Strictly logical analysis
   e.g., No. The writer does not say that he saw no unhealthy sprayed leaves

   ii Recognition of the ambiguity of the statement and looking for causes other than spraying to explain the phenomena. Often *implication* is understood in its more primitive form of equivalence (sh v $\overline{sh}$) (Peel, May 1967). This leads to an inability to accept the existence of unsprayed healthy leaves ($\bar{s}h$)

   e.g., No—as some of the unsprayed leaves were not

---

*The bar minus notation indicates the negation of a proposition.

diseased we cannot say definitely if the spray made the other leaves healthy

No—the fact that sprayed leaves were healthy may be just chance

iii Assuming that the problem was a statement of implication and that there were no unhealthy sprayed leaves. Support of this affirmation by reference to some or all of the four binary conjunctions

e.g., Yes—some definite effect—the sprayed leaves were healthy while the unsprayed ones were not all healthy

Yes—because the spray controlled the leaf disease where it had been used on the plants

iv In distinction from the first three categories of answers, all of which start from an awareness that the problem is largely logical, category iv answers do not reveal a reaction to the logical structure of the problem and are determined solely by the *content* that either some leaves were sprayed and others not *or* that the disease was not universal in the unsprayed leaves. The first fact led to assumptions about the act of spraying and by implications sometimes about the intention and effectiveness of the spray. The second led to comment about the nature of the disease. These answers are based on content as opposed to structure and may be linked with circumstantial answers.

e.g., Yes—the spray when applied to the leaves was effective to one and not the others

No—his friend could have missed, but it could mean it wasn't working.

v The residual of irrelevances, tautologies, inconsistencies, inability to comment and misunderstandings

e.g., No. Because he must know what he is doing

No. You have to spray your garden or the bugs will eat the leaves.

The frequencies in the different answer categories are given below:

Table XVIII

Answer categories	Main features	Postgraduate students	School pupils
i	logically adequate	25	1
ii	logical-causal looking for other causes	26	15
iii	assuming *implication* linguistic restriction	9	44
iv	content-circumstance dominated		10
v	restricted		14

Presumably we see here the effect of age and sophistication upon the power to cope with the logical and linguistic elements of a verbal problem situation. The answer categories bring out the various assumptions being made by the solver in relation to the logic and language of the passage.

CHAPTER FOUR

The Process of Making a Judgment

i THE COMPLETE ACT OF JUDGMENT

We have considered definitions of thinking and judging and have translated these ideas into operational means for stimulating and testing judgment. We have also described various factors which make for mature judgment and have reviewed experiments designed to reveal the extent of their influence during adolescence.

Now we study the act of judgment from its inceptions to completion and show, by similar experimental methods to those already described, how the various elements in the process show themselves over the period of adolescence. Briefly we shall investigate the arousal of the process, the imagination and formulation of hypotheses, and the selection and rejection of possibilities. This sequence of mental acts makes up the essentials of judging but it is also convenient to discuss as well what is meant by hypothetico-deductive reasoning since it enters particularly into the last stage of selecting an acceptable explanation and rejecting those not considered appropriate.

ii THE AROUSAL OF THE PROCESS

a Curiosity and interest

Any situation which provokes thought and judgment has in it an element of the unexpected—at the very least in the sense that the particular situation is one for which the thinker has no ready-made response. This element of the unexpected, incongruous, dissonant or cognitively out of equilibrium, sets off the motivation of the process of judging. There is apparently a large spontaneous element in the intellectual activity of most people and I wish to consider this and to look at it in terms of curiosity and interest. These are forces which seem intrinsic to processes of learning and thinking. We need to distinguish between the uninformed curiosity aroused by strange phenomena, objects and situations and the longer term-ideational curiosity (Peel, 1961) which impels and is impelled by the serious pursuit of understanding. From the latter emerge specialized knowledge-curiosities we call interests (Peel, 1958). These two—general knowledge-ideational curiosity and specific subject matter-curiosity or interest—seem most relevant.

Apparently, general curiosity is aroused maximally by partially familiar material and it is maintained by a balance of novelty and of material complexity. Novelty must pace complexity; otherwise curiosity may be killed. There is, in fact, a reciprocal interaction between curiosity and information which is set off by the joint action of complexity and novelty which results not only in the feedback of information but also of motivation.

A definite correlation has been demonstrated between the intel-

E

lectual-ideational curiosity aroused by a strange object and the number and quality of hypotheses put forward to explain it (Ashton, 1965). Ashton also investigated more thoroughly the effect of information given in connection with the objects. This was of four kinds:

- *i* Straightforward description of function which did not conflict with the child's comprehension of the subject
- *ii* Background information, also non-conflicting
- *iii* Conflicting statement of function
- *iv* No information given

Twelve pictures of museum objects were each presented with each piece of information and the effects of the four information-conditions were analysed against the curiosity aroused which was independently measured by frequency of choice.

When each child had seen all twelve pictures he was told that the experimenter had with her all of the actual objects that he had seen in the pictures. The child was then invited to choose those he would like to see and find out more about.

Ashton's main findings may be summarized as follows. Treating each single object as four separate ones according to each category of information with which it was presented, the following trends are marked. Objects presented with conflicting information predominate in the upper part of the popularity table and objects presented with a straightforward definition congregate toward the lower end. Objects presented with only background information or with no information at all are distributed fairly evenly through the table. The combination of object with conflicting information is appreciably more popular than the combination of object with definition.

A simple definition of function appeared to depress the curiosity which might have been expected on the basis of the overall popularity of the picture. Background information appeared to exercise no general effect possibly because its impact was highly dependent on the child's general knowledge. Objects presented with conflicting information aroused greatest interest.

The pertinence to curiosity of conflict and of strangeness enhanced by lack of information was underlined by the children's spontaneous responses. A frequent reason for wanting to know nore about a picture was stated to be its strangeness or unusual quality. The more curious the child, measured by the number of questions asked, the more frequently these reasons appeared.

Curiosity shows some remarkable interactions with novelty, complexity, nature of information and hypothesis formulation. It seems appropriate to describe it with interest as the instigator and maintainer of intellectual action.

Equilibration

Closely associated with the condition of curiosity is an urge to resolve the incongruities, inconsistencies and dissonances which give rise to the condition. At the level of ideational-curiosity the individual seems impelled to come to intellectual terms with his environment. Inhelder and Piaget (1958) go into the process of equilibration by breaking it down into the processes of assimilation and accommodation. Piaget later (1964) set forth this analysis very succinctly and I do not propose to repeat or discuss these sources.

What I would like to do is to put the concept of equilibrium in terms of the problems of explanation and judgment and perhaps to extend the idea a little.

In the acts of understanding and judging the child has to resolve a conflict between himself as a possessor of knowledge and his environment, which, by virtue of its unexpected elements, up to now unexperienced by him, constitutes for the thinker a disturbing situation. He seeks to remove this state of affairs by active resolution and compensation.

When a person *explains* a phenomenon he effects an equilibrium which is not stable in that better explanations may be forthcoming with more knowledge. However explanation is far more stable than description, which is relatively unstable because it does not relate an event or phenomenon to the wider context of knowledge. The equilibrium of description will always lead to that of explanation.

He can then go further, for once he can explain the situation to himself, he can then pass judgment against the background of his own previous experience.

Lastly, he is able to recognize conflicts and opposition within the material he studies—as in the maintenance of biological

ecologies, geographical environments, and social equilibria between
humans and animals.

iii PRELIMINARY EXPLORATION

Following quickly upon the arousal of intellectual interest and
indeed proceeding simultaneously with it is the preliminary survey
of the problem, where its features are discovered and linked
generally with the experience and insights of the thinker. This
process is so self-evident as to need little comment, save that it is
the graveyard of much problem solving. If the thinker finds the
situation intractable at this stage, he often appears too ready to
give up, for the merely partially analysed material seems to act as
a disproportionately powerful barrier.

iv IMAGINING AND FORMULATING HYPOTHESES

The characteristic of the highest level of answers, set out in Chapters 2 and 3 is that of conceiving of possible and hypothetical
contingencies. These had to be evoked from the thinker's experience
and insights. I call this feature of explaining and understanding
the imagined element. Formal thought implies a thinker capable of
imagining possibilities, conjured up in the form of generalizations,
concepts, analogies, cause-and-effect relations and such contingencies

In some of the test material described the passage and its
question were so designed as to evoke answers revealing a range of
imaginings, from those irrelevant, non-reality orientated, on to
limited but realistically tuned to the problem, finally to those
integrated, reasoned and taking account essentially of the problem.
Rhys (op. cit.) in connection with his soil erosion problem put the
following question:

> What could the farmer have done to prevent the destruction of
> his farmland?

This question calls for an imagined answer at all levels and the
purpose achieved is to bring out differences in the quality of the
imagined solutions. Apart from a few answers in which the pupils
showed that they were incapable of invoking any ideas at all, the
bulk of responses are well represented by the following sample,

divided into four groups revealing improving quality.

i By watering the soil every day.

He could have dug down and got the rock out of the ground before he started to sow.

He could have put fertilizers down.

Antonio was not a good farmer. If he had not cut the trees down they would have kept the ground fertile.

To prevent the destruction of his farmland he could have left the big trees up because they would have kept his soil fertile.

ii He could have re-seeded his pasture and made thicker grass. He could also have taken less land and expanded later on. He could also have changed to rye which doesn't need such a rich soil.

To prevent the destruction of his field A. shouldn't have cut down all the trees. He should have cut down a few at a time.

He could have put wooden banks on the side of the river. Build a dam and have less water running down.

He could have left some of the trees in the group and left most of the tree stumps in the ground also. Then the ground would have been fertile and the soil would not have been washed away, because the tree stumps would have held the soil.

iii If A. had cut down some of his trees and then left a border all the way around the wind and rain couldn't have blown or washed the soil away. By this A. would have been able to go on farming.

If he planted the harvest in different places every year the moisture would have stayed, but he used the ground too many times, so the moisture had gone.

iv A. could have done much to prevent these things happening. If he had made a suitable dam before the rain came the water would have been trapped. He then could have used the water sparingly throughout the hotter months. He could have had a consistent water supply year after year in this way.

If A. used his head, which he did not, he could have saved his land and become a prosperous farmer. If he had used the yearly cycle by rotating his crops, his land could have been very good for potatoes, maize, wheat and corn. If in winter he stored his water in a well instead of letting it flow down the hill and into the ground he would have never been out of water either.

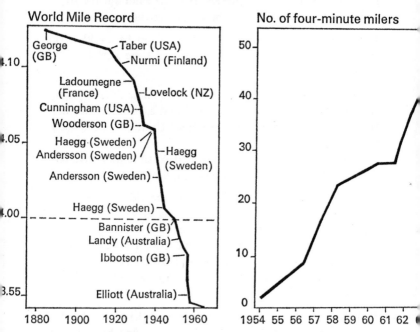

Fig. 3 THE LEFT-HAND graph shows how the world mile record has fallen this century — breaking the four-minute barrier exactly ten years ago. Since then an average of four or five runners a year have entered the ranks of four-minute milers: the steadily increasing total is shown on the right-hand graph. Herb Elliott has performed the feat most often (17 times), and altogether it has been done 129 times on outdoor tracks and 12 times on indoor tracks (one further claim is disputed). Last year was the best ever with 36 sub-four-minute miles, which means that a feat that was regarded as 'impossible' only ten years ago is now performed at an average of once every ten days. The present record (3 min. 54.5 sec.) was set in 1962 by Peter Snell.

(The *Sunday Times*, London 10 May, 1964, reproduced by kind permission.)

Besides the quality of the imagined explanation psychologists and educationalists are interested in the *number* of imaginings, the assumption being that a creative mind may perceive many possible causes. Much of this work stemmed from Guilford's original concept (1956) of divergent thinking. I do not propose to survey this research nor have we used the type of test customary in research on divergent thinking. We have tended to devise verbal anecdotal material or demographic data permitting of a wide range of explanation.

Here is an example of the latter which brings out wide differences in the number of imaginings in relation to age (13–20).

Given the graphs opposite and statistics about four-minute milers, one asks for possible causes of the lowering of the time for running the mile and of the growing numbers of runners who perform the feat year by year.

The following list of possible explanations are given for two persons, who were also asked, as done by Frederiksen (1959), to state what further information would be required to prove or disprove each cause put forward.

Person A (aged 14)—two possible explanations—no answers to the second part of the question.

  i Firstly the record has improved because the people have something to beat and so they try harder.

  ii The athletes got better ways of training as time went on.

Person B (aged 16) seven possible explanations matched by seven pieces of information required.

  i People might be fitter and healthier today than before with better food, etc.

  ii Perhaps sport is taken more seriously today and more training is being done.

  iii Perhaps men are changing physically, i.e. becoming taller, or slimmer or more well built for running.

  iv Perhaps weather conditions are better, i.e., (a) more chance for training and (b) less wind to run against.

  v Tracks are in better condition and so easier to run on, perhaps.

  vi Perhaps running gear, i.e., shorts, spiked shoes, etc., are better, lighter to run in.

vii Perhaps gains are better so there is more incentive to run, i.e., bigger prizes.

To prove

1. What food was like before and is like now, and how fit they were compared to how fit they are now,
2. How much training they used to do before and how much they do today,
3. What the average runner was like in build in 1952 compared to the runner today,
4. The weather conditions in general in 1954 and the general weather conditions of today; also what the weather was like on the days that the athletes ran in 1964 and 1954,
5. The conditions of the tracks then and now,
6. What running gear was like then and what it is like now,
7. The amount of money spent on prizes in 1954 and in 1964.

Davies (1964) devised anecdotal material, including the following test items:

a During 5 years at school John Brown held the following positions in class at the end of the year:

| 4th | 3rd | 1st | 20th | 12th |

Give as many reasons as you can that would explain the sudden change.

b An owner of a Public House and Off-Licence kept a record of his takings for a period of eight weeks. Suggest as many reasons as you can for the sudden increase in takings during the fifth and sixth weeks.

Week	1	2	3	4	5	6	7	8
Takings	£56	£49	£53	£57	£94	£87	£48	£52

c A policeman stopped Joe Lightfinger at one o'clock in the morning as he was walking along the High Street. Joe was carrying a large bag of tools. The policeman was suspicious. What possible explanations could Joe offer the policeman?

The answers offered to these questions from two extreme individuals were as follows:

a He didn't study enough. Was not worried after being top. The work was much too hard for him. He didn't pay much attention to the teacher. Used to stargaze during the lessons.

a Illness, accident, absence, harder work, cleverer people came into the class, did not work hard, put in a higher class, did not learn his work, did not do homework, class got larger, did not understand the work, had a different teacher who did not teach so well, lost his writing arm.

b People having celebration, holiday, people on tour.

b Rich visitors, carnival week, a lot of visitors arrived, large celebration, lot of marriages, unusual spirits in stock, lots of holiday makers and tourists, good weather therefore more customers, he offered stamps for two weeks.

c With friends at their houses missed the last bus home — they were his mate's tools which he had borrowed.

c Going to mend burst pipes, with his friend's tools, going to mend friend's burst pipes. Coming home from a party he stayed over at, after working late — left them at a friend's house and needed them for work — returning them to a plumber friend.

A perusal of these answers shows that a count of numbers of ideas cannot be taken as a sole measure of inventiveness, for some of the suggestions are not realistically related to the problem. After such unacceptable answers had been pruned out, the number of explanations obtained from 50 children correlated with the Heim AH4 Group Test of general intelligence to the extent of .52, using the rank order coefficient.

It will be apparent from the instances given, that the imagination must be coherent and articulate so that the possibilities offered as explanations can be formulated and communicated. Without this condition we could not assess the imagination and creativity of the thinker.

v SELECTING THE MOST APPROPRIATE AND REJECTING THE LESS EFFECTIVE HYPOTHESES

Only very rarely do people have real initial difficulty in offering some sort of explanation of an event or phenomenon and can usually pass judgment on it without much trouble. But once a particular hypothesis has been devised or accepted by the thinker he seems to have somewhat greater difficulty in shifting to another.

This difficulty shows itself in two ways. First the thinker is more likely to try to hold on to his first view—even if he has to modify it—in the face of new observations and experimental results. This is not a tendency of immature thinkers only, but is a characteristic of the most sophisticated and informed intellectuals. When the weight of evidence from observation and experiment reaches such proportion that no more modification to the initial theory can cope with it, then there is a change of hypothesis. The history of science can be equated with such a process of formation, modification and change of theories. I think we have to keep this feature of hypothesis formation in mind when we consider the difficulties encountered by adolescents and adults in taking up new lines of thought to explain problem situations.

The second way in which new explanations may be obstructed is by the directive and selective influence of the accepted theory upon the subsequent collection of observations and results. People, even learned ones, may tend to look for what supports their theory and consciously or unconsciously neglect evidence which contradicts it.

When Hotson (1964) brought out his hypothesis that Shakespeare's Mr W.H. of the Sonnets was William Hatcliffe, critics of his view, which was largely supported, among other evidence, by the incidence of cryptogramic plays on the parts of the name, HAT, LIFFE, LIFE, LIVE, etc., in the Sonnets, as in

But were some childe of yours alive tHAT time,
You should LIVE twise in it, and in my rime, HATLIVE
(Sonnet 17)

were quick to point out the selective nature of this evidence and of other possibilities.

...The many references to t(hat) and life or live in the Sonnets, to Hatcliffe's arms of three primroses, or 'True-Loves', to his being a 'king' are plausible but prove nothing; nor does the Hilliard miniature. Like all who operate on these problems Dr Hotson selects the quotations which assist his theories and neglects the others. (For example, *Willobie his Avisa.*) It will be my turn next. I have my anagram ready:

'William Shakespeare': 'Speaker is lame awhil(e)'. There are three references to lameness in the Sonnets though whether lame as a duck or as an excuse is not yet clear to me. It will be.

(Connolly, 1964.)

A year later another controversial theory, turning on the origin of the Vinland map (Marston *et al.*, 1965), evoked similar suggestions of partiality in recognizing the evidence (*Sunday Times*, 6 March 1966).

It seems that it may be inadequate and misleading to talk of observations as objectively unassailable data, since they may be partial and selected as a result of direction by the hypothesis held. They may be better described as *hypothetico-observations* in the sense that we talk of hypothetico-deductions, where deduction follows from a hypothesis. Similarly, in the second kind of obstruction to further theorizing, we have observations following upon and influenced by the theories held by the observer.

Small wonder that the testing of hypothesis and the elimination of those less effective make up severe tests of adolescent and adult thinking. As we have seen people are usually too ready to continue to infer a particular belief from evidence which would also support another. In one research carried out by Wason (1960) students had to find the concept of *three numbers in increasing order* by putting up sets of three numbers for judgment by the experimenter, who of course knew the concept. The most frequent responses were positive instances enumerated to illustrate the concept chosen. Relatively few sets were chosen to eliminate alternative concepts, and also few negative instances deliberately chosen to test the assumed concept. If for instance the experimenter starts off with even number sequences: 2, 4, 10; 18, 16, 20; 38, 100, 150, etc., the subjects, having formed the concept *3 even numbers* are likely to persist in setting up sets of even numbers *confirming* their assumption rather than putting up other sequences 3, 4, 9, etc., to *test* it. Wason concluded: very few intelligent young adults spontaneously test their beliefs in a situation which does not appear to be of a 'scientific' nature.

This tendency seems to be true whatever the kind of explanation involved; contingency of events, cause and effect, or reference to more abstract concepts.

In more general terms it is essential in experiments designed to investigate the effect or presence of certain phenomena in relation to other conditions to include a control where the conditions are absent or negative.

In his study on the judgments of pupils of average ability aged 14–15 years Davies (*op. cit.*) asked a question in which three alternative hypotheses were given from which the pupils had to select the most appropriate one.

The question followed a brief but comprehensive comment on the factors entering into the choice of location of industry. These were: land, labour, new materials, power, markets and transport presented as follows:

A number of factors influence a business man when he decides where to start a new factory or workshop. The following are the most important:

LAND. He must be able to rent or buy land in sufficient amounts and as cheaply as possible. The more land that is needed the cheaper it must be.

LABOUR. There must be people available to work in his factory. Some jobs need people who are very skilled, while others can be done by anyone. If skilled labour is needed then the factory is likely to be built where such people are already living. When only unskilled labour is needed a factory may be built near any big town.

RAW MATERIALS. Some industries use a lot of heavy raw materials and so it pays to site them near the source of supply if this is possible, rather than pay the high transport costs. For this reason the iron and steel industry is often found near coal or iron ore deposits. Industries that use only a little raw material are not tied to their source of supply. Some industries depend on the products of others for their raw materials and are frequently located near these supplying industries.

POWER. Industries using a lot of coal tend to choose sites near the coalfields to save transport costs. It is easier and cheaper to transport fuel oil and electricity and so industries depending on these are less tied to the source of their supply.

MARKETS. It pays a manufacturer to be as near as

possible to the market where he sells his products, especially when they are bulky, difficult to handle or liable to be broken or damaged during transportation.

TRANSPORT. The bulkier the goods and the greater the distances, the higher the cost of transport will tend to be. However, some means of transport are cheaper than others, but usually slower. Ocean and canal transport are cheaper than the rest but are slowest. Railways are faster but more expensive. Road transport is faster still but is unsuited to really bulky loads and is the most costly. Air transport which is very expensive is suitable only for people and light valuable merchandise which must be transported urgently.

It is very rare for a manufacturer to be able to satisfy all these conditions when choosing a site, but he will try and satisfy as many as possible. Before he can choose a site he must decide which of these factors is most important in his case and so a man who needs to employ a large labour force but needs little raw material will choose a site near a big town even if this means transporting the raw materials many miles.

The question asked was:

Which of the following would worry an industrialist most:

    a an increase in his wages bill,

    b an increase in transport costs,

    c an increase in rent.

Only one pupil out of 50 considered all three alternatives, his reply being:

I think an increase in wages, because he's got to pay his men every week and the rent isn't so high—but it's there all the time and the transport costs might be high and then low because they might be sending their goods to a near town and then next week to one a bit further away.

Five pupils considered two alternatives:

It all depends really how big his factory is. If it wasn't a very big factory he could afford to increase the wages and if he had to get a lot of raw materials sent in that would be more expensive for him.

Thirty-nine considered only one possibility and neglected to mention any other:

Increase in rent. (Why?) 'Cos if he wanted to expand he would have to pay more for the land.
Increase in transport costs. (Why?) Well he's got lots of goods to be delivered and it would cost more than if the pay went up or the rent.
In wages. (Why?) They might go on strike otherwise.
Transport costs. (Why?) The cost of transport is already very expensive.

The remaining five were incapable of supporting their assertions:

Increase in transport bill. (Why?) I can't think of any reasons.
Wages. (Why?) I don't know.

Here we see that average mid-adolescents are rarely capable of dealing overtly with problems involving selection and elimination of hypotheses, even when those hypotheses are given to them and all the supporting evidence is provided. It might be argued that absence of mention of the two less preferred alternatives is no evidence that they have not been considered. This criticism however would have more weight if Davies had not used an individual spoken interview technique.

In another investigation, Mealings (1961, 1963) revealed the difficulties encountered by mid-adolescents in dealing spontaneously with simple practical science problems requiring the choice of a correct hypothesis and the rejection of incorrect ones.

In one problem the pupils were told that there were possible only two alternatives, one of which was correct. The problem required the investigation of a white powder (actually consisting of a mixture of salt and chalk), given water and hydrochloric acid, to find out if it was *one* substance or *two*. The necessary apparatus for dissolving, filtering and evaporating was also supplied. Each of 57 pupils carried out the experiment individually and full records were kept of what each did and said.

Group 0
Random Trial and Error tests—no logical process made—

experiments done in the hope that something would turn up. Observations correctly reported but not related to any organized system of thought. No hypotheses formulated, no valid deductions made. Fail to realize that filtrate (after water added) may contain a dissolved substance.

Group 1

Separated salt from chalk by water and filtering, each saw possibility of filtrate containing a dissolved salt but could not translate this into a practical solution by evaporating. Some said two because HCL dissolves, water does not (this is not a solution).

Group 2

Separated by shaking with water and evaporating filtrate— assumed two substances—none considered possibility that substance was *one*, freely soluble in acid, moderately soluble in water. None thought of using HCL to test the two residues— though HCL not necessary.

Group 3

Separated, saw the possibility that the substance was single and used acid on the two residues to demonstrate effervescence and non-effervescence.

The results were as follows:

Table XIX

Category of performance	n	Median mental age	Range of mental age
0	37	14+	11+ – 17+
1	8	17	13+ – 18+
2	9	17+	15+ – 18+
3	3	18+	all at 18+

Mealings does not say how many were put off by starting off with hydrochloric acid, which might in fact slow up subsequent progress. But setting this possibility aside, we see that few were able

to proceed beyond the first separation by shaking with water and
filtering, at which stage the alternative hypothesis had to be
formulated and tested, by first evaporating and then considering
whether the two solids, that left on the filter paper and that produced by evaporating the filtrate, were one and the same or different (by using the acid provided).

The above experiment does not call for combinatorial thinking
(Inhelder and Piaget, 1958, Chapters 6 and 7), that is, the systematic trying out of combinations of substances. Such thinking i
a feature of hypothesis elimination when there are several alternatives composed of conjunctions of different phenomena.

The second experiment I want to report from Mealing's work
was concerned with this problem and its methods and results con-
formed with the similar experiment of Inhelder and Piaget which
suggested it. The problem requires only a knowledge of the distinction between a chemical change and a physical mixture.

Each subject was provided with five clear colourless liquids contained in corked conical flasks and labelled A, B, C, D and E
respectively. The contents of the flasks were as follows:

A—water + phenolphthalein
B—limewater
C—sodium carbonate solution
D—limewater
E—calcium chloride solution

The subject was informed that two of the flasks contained the same
kind of liquid and was asked to carry out tests, in the test tubes
provided, in order to find out which two flasks contained identical
solutions. To solve the problem, it was necessary for him to carry
out a systematic sequence of binary combinations.

It will be appreciated that the identical liquids would (a) not
react with one another, (b) react similarly with other reagents. One
solution would be as follows:

Begin by mixing A with each of the other liquids in turn

	with	B	C	D	E
Mix					no
A		red	red	red	change

therefore A ≠ B, C, D and E ≠ B, C, D

Now mix E with B, C, D.

with	B	C	D
Mix	no	white	no
E	change	ppt	change

Therefore $A \neq E$ by virtue of their different reactions with B and $B \neq C$, $C \neq D$ by virtue of different reactions with E.

Of the 10 possible mixtures of A, B, C, D, E, two at a time, all but B, D have resulted in unidentical pairs.

Therefore $B = D$.

A subject might begin by mixing B, C, D or E with each of the other reagents in turn. The reagents were chosen in such a way that this would make very little difference to the difficulty of the problem. In each case a similar pattern of inferences would emerge.

Results

Group O

Nine subjects in this group attempted to solve the problem by simply inspecting the clear liquids. After prompting, some mixed the liquids, but not systematically. After some initial binary combinations, tertiary and other more complex mixing were undertaken but apparently without any clear purpose.

Group 1

These subjects all carried out some systematic binary combinations and attempted to draw inferences from their results. Their conclusions were invalid, because they were based upon unsufficient evidence. For example, one pupil immediately terminated her investigation when two reagents failed, when mixed, to produce any observable change. She inferred that 'no reaction on mixing' inevitably meant that the two reagents were identical. In fact, this was only a possible explanation.

Group 2

In this group the subjects all systematically investigated sufficient binary combinations for a successful solution of the problem. The

F

subjects were, however, unable to make full use of the information which they obtained. For example, a girl began by mixing A with B, C, D and E respectively. She then investigated the possibility that A was the same as E. She did not, however, deduce that since B, C and D all reacted similarly with A, the following possibilities also existed: B = C, B = D, C = D.

'You are not given anything else?' (No.) She inspects the liquids in the flasks. 'I will test each of them with A.'

    A + B – red coloration
    A + C – red coloration
    A + D – red coloration
    A + E – nil 'What do I have to find?'

(Which two flasks contain the same liquid?) 'I will test B, C and D with E.'

    B + E – nil
    C + E – milky
    D + E – nil
    A + E – nil 'B and D both give red with A and remain clear with E. But so did A (i.e., A remained clear with E). I will try B with each one.'

    B + A – red coloration
    B + D – nil
    B + E – nil 'B with E and D remain clear.' (Have you any idea which two are the same?) 'D and E.' (E – why?) 'B, C and D give red with A. Gosh! A and B give red, but B and E, and B and D remain clear.'

Group 3

These subjects all successfully solved the problem. They proceeded systematically, setting up and testing hypotheses and making valid inferences from their results. On the other hand, they each carried out more binary mixings than was absolutely necessary for a strictly logical solution of the problem. Here is such a solution.

'I will see how they react together. I will try A and B first.'

    A + B – red
    A + C – red
    A + D – red
    A + E – nil 'A makes B, C and D mauve, but not E. A and

E may be the same. I will see if E makes the others go mauve as well.'

E + B – nil

E + C – milky

E + D – nil 'A and E are not the same. Now I will see if A and D are the same'.

D + B – nil 'D is not the same as A. I will try whether A and C are the same.'

C + B – white precipitate. 'C is not the same as A. I will see what C does to E.'

C + E white precipitate. 'It looks as if C makes everything go milky.'

A + C – red 'A and C are not the same.' Pause. 'None of them are the same as A or C. It is two out of B, D and E. But E does not react with A in the same way as B and D do. Therefore B and D are the same.'

Group 4

A single subject used rigorous logical analysis in order to solve the problem by the most direct method, i.e., the method requiring the minimum number of binary combinations.

'Have I any other reagents?' (E – No. Only the liquids in the flasks.) He pours a little liquid from each flask into a clean test-tube. He then adds a little of B to each.

B + A – red

B + B – nil

B + C – white precipitate

B + D – nil

B + E – nil 'A and C react differently from one another, so we may eliminate those.' He pushes the flasks containing A and C to one side. He pours a little of B, D and E into each of three test-tubes. 'Now which one shall I add . . . I will use A.'

A + B – red

A + D – red

A + E – nil 'B and D react similarly with A, so B and D are the same.'

The complete analysis of the whole group of pupils gave the following results:

Table XX

Category of solution	n	Median M.A.	Range of M.A.
0	12	12+	11+ – 16+
1	18	14+	13+ – 16+
2	14	16+	14+ – 18+
3	11	16+	14+ – 18+
4	1	18+	

The chief results of interest here are

a the relative incapacity of the children to make the logical requirements effective by either not being able to use the information they had acquired (Category 2) or by gathering too much (Category 3) or not gathering enough (Category 1).

b the incapacity of some children to see that conjunction or mixing was required.

c absence of systematic trials.

d as in Mealing's first experiment again we see inability to conceive of alternative hypotheses and to eliminate them by appropriate testing (all that was required was to find two liquids which did not react together and which reacted in the same way with other agents).

The elimination of alternative hypotheses proves so difficult in the type of experimental setting described that one is prompted to ask whether this is due solely to the artificiality of the situations used. I think not. I have tried in chemistry and history lessons to evoke alternatives without a great deal of success. Teachers at all levels tend to streamline the learning process by presenting the most acceptable hypothesis and neglecting to eliminate the remainder. While this may be justified on some grounds and a full consideration of all alternatives rejected with equal weight, teachers should not forget that it is part of their task to promote thinking and that the complete act of selecting a best judgment entails rejecting the others. To this end they might more often draw attention to alternate explanations in order that the pupils may themselves reject them.

As we have seen, scholars and scientists tend to seize upon an acceptable hypothesis and proceed by modification. Also where the evidence is mixed there is a related tendency to look at that which supports the accepted thesis. There is an organic quality in the development of a thesis as opposed to a clear-cut process of logical elimination. Also, in science particularly, there are often only two alternatives, mutually excluded and excluding, and positive support for one view implies rejection of the other. The thinker does not have to go beyond the positive thinking required. There may also be a mental inertia which predisposes a person to neglect to clear away the alternatives. Lastly we judge things in our environment generally be their positive presence. It is not the way to proceed by eliminating what is negative—rather we look for what is extant, evident and tangible.

vi HYPOTHETICO-DEDUCTIVE REASONING

a Its ubiquity

If we had worked systematically through all the possible mixtures of two liquids in the problem involving five simple chemicals we should still have not been able to identify the identical pair merely by the acts of mixing and enumeration. We would have had, for instance, the following table of results from systematic pairings of A with B, C and E, C with D, E... etc.

Table XXI

Aqueous solutions		A	B	C	D	E
Phenolphthalein	A		red	red	red	nil
limewater	B			white ppt	nil	nil
sodium carbonate	C				white ppt	white ppt
limewater	D					nil
Calcium chloride	E					

We have four possible identical pairings: AE, BD, BE and DE. And we can find which pair consists of identical substances (B and D) only by further action by reasoning deductively from the entries in the above table against the setting of the two premises:

  i The two identical substances do not react with each other;

  ii They react in a similar way with any third substance.

As we have seen in the last section, if we make use of our deductive machinery as soon as we have tried out a complete row of pairings we can in fact reduce the number of experimental pairings required to find the two identical substances.

We may note the deductive processes at work in the reported schedules of the actual attempts made by pupils to find the identical pair of liquids.

The deductive element is also quite apparent in all the other instances of making judgments utilized in the last section. Generally there is scarcely a single problem situation described in this book which does not involve at least one deduction for a formal comprehensive solution.

b Induction and deduction

The differences between induction and deduction relate closely to those between description and explanation.

An inductive process begins with particular instances and from them reaches a rule or generalization which covers them all. Often this rule will also cover fresh instances not used to induce it, but this cannot be assumed as a necessary consequence. The induction of the rule for the number of games played in knockout championships (Chapter 1) has been mentioned. Here is another:

> Put a point on the circumference of a circle. Now put on another. Join the points with a straight line. Now put on another, joining all the points with straight lines. Add other points and join them up with straight lines. Induce the general rule connecting the number of points and the number of straight lines joining them.

Seven points provides 21 lines, 8, 28 etc. Inducing the rule in this

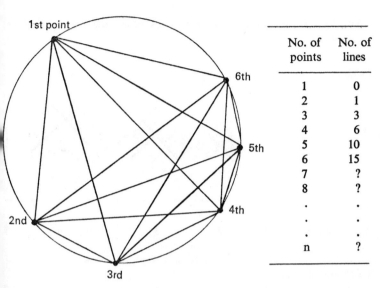

No. of points	No. of lines
1	0
2	1
3	3
4	6
5	10
6	15
7	?
8	?
.	.
.	.
.	.
n	?

Figure 4

case is not so easy for younger pupils. The rule is: for n points there are

$$\frac{n^2-n}{2} \text{ lines.}$$

The relation of induction to description is clear from these instances. Induction enables one to describe the features of a phenomenon by means of a single rule. This rule however is not related to wider implications nor necessarily to the conceptual structure of the problem. One can however 'structure' the induction to lead to a real insight, as done in the following instance I used both for testing the mathematical powers of 10 year olds and also as a means for teaching. It is in fact a very short programme of instruction and testing.

Structural instructions

In the following table we are going to build up squares from a small square by adding similar squares along the top two edges, as shaded.

Table XXII

Number of small squares along one side	1	2	3	4	5
Total number of small squares in larger square	1	4	9	16	?
How the squares grow	1	1+1+1+1	4+2+2+1	9+3+3+1	?

Now do the following:

Complete the 5-square by drawing it in the blank space in the top row of the table.

Fill in the table the total number of small squares in it.

Fill in the bottom row of the table to show how this 5-square has grown from a 4-square.

Imagine you have to make a 7-square from a 6-square. Write down here, as in the bottom row of the table, how a 7-square would grow from a 6-square.

In the same way if $32 \times 32 = 1024$, show how you can tell me what 33×33 is without multiplying these numbers out.

Can you state the rule in words by which any sized square grows into the next bigger square?

Some phenomena are capable of treatment only by induction—and this goes often for events which at first we do not understand. So we may induce the weather likely or the prices on the Stock Exchange or the chances of a particular horse winning the Derby. If later a science of meteorology or investment develops, then we may not have to depend exclusively on induction.

Where it permits of application, deduction is a far more effective tool in that it related the phenomena to general principles or to independent antecedent events tied by a necessary relationship with those being investigated. There is first an extension of the principle to include the case in hand. Thus a deductive process provides a proof which is also in effect an explanation, as shown in the two-line proof of the knockout competition outlined in Chapter 1.

Applying the same method to the problem about the number of points on a circle and the number of straight lines joining them, we would first note the essential structure of the problem, that if there were n points, the first point would join to $(n-1)$ joints, the second to $(n-2)$, since its join to the first point has already been counted, the third to $(n-3)$, the rth to $(n-r)$, the $n-1^{th}$ to one point, the nth to no point. (Note that this structure is far more general than in the circle problem—it is the basis of the number of binary conjunctions between a number of elements, as shown for example in the chemicals problem on p. 85.) Having analysed the problem structurally into more general terms, all we need to do is to sum the arithmetical progression consisting of the n terms

$$0, 1, 2, \ldots\ldots (n-1), \ldots\ldots (n-2) \ (n-1)$$

$$\text{which is } \frac{n(n-1)}{2}$$

Deduction then is an explanatory tool far outweighing the description technique of induction. Indeed in some mathematics games—as in geometrical riders—satisfying progress is made only by deduction.

The real difficulty for the younger and middle adolescent pupil is to cross the bridge from induction to deduction. But the inductive method must not be despised, nor can it be dispensed with. It enables one to soften up a problem, to map out likely deductive proofs for new and unfamiliar phenomena.

c Deducing from hypotheses

When we turn from mathematics to situations involving empirical data, as in science, geography and in the comprehension problems reported in Chapters 2 and 3, we find that the hypothesis or possibility takes on a clearer role in the deductive process. This is true whether it is put as an explanation or basis of a judgment or is a statement of the end results of a science experiment.

Any offered hypothesis has to be justified by deductive reasoning against the actual features and contents of the situation it purports to explain, as in the problems devised by Valentine (1954) to measure higher level intelligence.

Similarly one can shift the emphasis in the analysis of judgment to that of investigating the deductive processes involved. This is done by providing the thinker with a proposition to examine against the information supplied in the test. In these circumstances he does not have to invoke an explanation but rather to examine one. Rhys used this technique with insight and effect when he provided the pupil with demographic charts setting out the problem facing crofter farmers in the Isle of Lewis. No text was used but maps were provided showing the essential geographical features of the island and bringing out the generally poor quality of the land. Charts were also provided, showing the proportion and nature of crops as against pasture and the number of sheep and cattle. Rainfall and temperature charts were also included.

The proposition to be examined was put in the question form:

Are the crofters making the best use of their land by growing crops only over such a small area?

In order to answer this question satisfactorily, the thinker has to resolve the conflict between the land apparently available and unused and its quality, and he needs to consider the grazing habits of the animals. This calls for deductive argument.

Analysis of the answers brings out evidence of a wide range of deductive power among adolescents.

 i Personal, tautological answers.
  'Yes, because they've got the beauty of the deer in the forest.'
  'They're making good use of their land.'

 ii Seizure of *one* piece of visual evidence.
  'If they didn't have so many animals, they could have more crops.'

 iii The beginnings of taking account of more than one factor.

'Yes, because he does not need too many crops. The more pasture he has the better his sheep and cattle are fed.'

iv A detailed, systematic appraisal of the difficulties presented to the crofters by their restricted environment.

'The crofters are sensible in growing only a few crops over a little area because the ground is mainly mountains and very rough. It would be hard to get the necessary amount of crops needed to feed the crofters, the only crops which they have cultivated with a little success are the hardier, tougher crops, oats and potatoes. The land can be made of better use by rough grazing with sheep on the hills and mountains.'

This top category of answers, characteristic of the older and abler members of the group tested, included the following responses:

Yes. I think they are quite right in applying the policy as, in addition to the fact that the common pasture is of poor quality, to farm extensively the whole area would engage the costly business of clearing the comparatively large deer forest. Clearly their best policy is being practical, and to nearly ignore the poor ground, and taking to the sea where a richer crop of whale, salmon and other common sea fish can be obtained. If crop farming was extensively practised, the harvesting would also be a big headache, as the harvesting months of October and September are among the months with the highest rainfall, very unfavourable for harvesting crops. Lastly if farming was practised, the few males there would have difficulty in finding work, as the island is very small in itself, and they may have to go to the mainland to find it.

I think they are using their land to full extent because what they can't grow, they can get by selling the fish that they catch, to other places far inland who cannot fish for their own fish. Also on the rough ground they can graze their cattle and sheep from which they can obtain milk and also meat. From the milk they can make their own butter and cheese. What cereals and vegetables cannot be grown, can be imported from nearby Scotland.

Yes, they are sensible in growing only a little food, because where they live is mainly poor mountainous farmland and it would be very hard to plough the land without machinery, supposing these people don't have machinery. Anyway the land which is made into crops and grass is very good land, but the other parts we are told is only poor quality, ill-drained with acres of rock and peat on it. A large number of men are regularly away and if the farmers tried to put out a bigger output of crops he might not find the labour.

The crofters are being sensible in only having small areas of crops because the common pasture is of poor quality, ill-drained with areas of rock and peat. The composition of the croft areas are part of grass, sown grass, oats and potatoes, and this encourages them with crops and livestock, which has many sheep and about 40 cattle. The rainfall is less heavy in those croft areas than in the common pasture and if you notice it on the map, the croft areas are situated near the sea which allows the rainwater to be drained into the sea more easily. Also of course they are in a position to use fishing as another important income. Good farming would be impossible in the common pasture of these people in the island of Lewis off the NW of Scotland.

In each of these responses we have evidence of ability to weigh the suggestion against the elements of the actual environment in which the crofters live—particularly those which restrict the action of the farmers and where there is a conflict between the quality and amount of land available.

The chronological and mental ages associated with these categories of the deductive process are as follows, ages given in months:

Table XXIII

Categories	Chronological age			Mental age (Raven)	
	n	m	SD	n	SD
i	13	127·3	8·9	130·9	18·8
ii	31	142·4	10·5	150·0	13·4
iii	37	159·2	11·2	169·9	17·3
iv	39	181·5	8·7	192·8	19·5

We note that not before the age of 15 can we expect to obtain systematic and coherent deductive argument.

The hypothetico-deductive method is often used in developing ideas and fresh conclusions in physics under the name of 'thought experiments' (Miller, 1959). There is, however, a potential danger in such 'armchair' science. Since 'thought experiments' dispense with real action and experimentation their weakest point is in the possibly unwarranted assumptions made of what happens phenomenally or in actual practice. These then lead to false or limited deductions. Thus Aristotle predicted that a needle would sink and a piece of paper float on the basis of what he knew about density. The prediction is a simple form of thought experiment. But there are other phenomena involved, as Galileo showed, one being surface tension and wetting of surfaces. When the experiment is *actually tried*, the needle floats and the paper sinks as Galileo demonstrated. Here the force of surface tension counteracts the force of gravity.

Another instance was that of Aristotle's 'proof' that a vacuum could not exist. His reasoning went as follows:

a He begins with a generalization that of two similar moving bodies that which is in the denser medium will move more slowly, e.g., a stone falling in water moves more slowly than a similar one in air.

b His next generalization following from the first is that, other things being equal, speed is inversely proportional to the density of the medium.

c It is axiomatic that the density of a vacuum is zero. From c and b he deduces that the velocity of a vacuum is infinitely great which means that a body would be in two places at once. But a body cannot be in two places at once. Therefore a vacuum cannot exist.

Aristotle failed to prove generalization b by experiment. Again we are reminded that action, here by experiment, is the basis of thought and is the safeguard against the intrusion of unwarranted assumptions.

This excerpt was used by Whellock (1952) as one item in a test of scientific reasoning and asked his subjects, all either sixth form pupils or military cadets, the following question:

Aristotle's mistake which led him to a wrong conclusion was:

a The ratio of the density of a vacuum to the density of any other medium cannot be expressed by a number, since zero divided by any number is infinitely small.

b It does not follow that an object with infinite velocity is in two places at once.

c His first two generalizations refer to media, whereas a vacuum is not a medium and therefore generalizations *a* and *b* cannot apply.

d He failed to prove his second generalization by means of experiments.

e None of the above.

Only sixteen per cent of his subjects selected answer *d* and the results from his test as a whole revealed the difficulties presented by hypothetico-deductive problems. Valentine (1954) tested sixth form and university student groups and found similar severities. All this confirms the opinions expressed earlier in this chapter that reasoning from hypotheses is a most sophisticated thought form calling for experience and intellectual maturity in the thinker.

In the humanities the need for hypothetico-deduction is no less necessary or demanding. It often appears in historical explanation and literary criticism in the form of what is called conducting a 'sustained argument'. The most mature answers quoted on page 91 in response to the crofter problem show some evidence of this quality. It was brought out clearly in a study of grammar school girls' reasoning in history (Peel, Second Edition, pp. 122–5, 1968) which revealed the very marked gradient by age in the power and sophistication of such thinking.

Making an intellectual judgment then calls for several capabilities:

explicit formulation of possible explanations or hypotheses,

linked with a capacity to hold an argument through long examinations of the situation involved;

a mastery of language in relation to reason (Chapter 3, Section v),

detection of inconsistencies and partialities;

relating the situational facts to the offered hypothesis;

selection and rejection of possibilities;

and examining a situation formally and structurally as against circumstantially and merely by content.

CHAPTER FIVE

Insight into the Dynamics of Stability and Change

i VARIABILITY IN THE ENVIRONMENT

The stars at night, the topography of the earth and the living kingdom all bear witness to the permanence and the variability of our environment. Humanity seeks to give meaning to this variability by looking for what is stable and for what is changing and by analysing the nature and conditions of such stability and transience. Although this way of looking at nature is so self-evident to the adult that the twofold scheme appears to be a characteristic of nature, when we come to study its finer points, we realize how much it is a way of man's responding to his environment. In particular we find in the formative years of childhood and adolescence that ideas of stability and change do not appear ready made but develop gradually.

The first thing we notice about existential stability is that it is only partially static. The stability we call good health or an adequate standard of living is a state of balance achieved by a process of action and counter-action or give and take. When we examine the element of change in time we see that it is not always continuous nor undirectional nor regular. We may have good and bad times. Some processes of change lead to a more organized state of affairs, others to degeneration and distintegration.

Viewed in this way, both stability and variation with time are based on the concept of change. Equilibrium, resulting in stability, is achieved by compensating change with change. Thus in the case of biological and geographical ecology the equilibrium is maintained by the interrelatedness of living organisms, plants and animals, in the biotic community in cycles of energy, matter and food. No organism lives alone. Species interact with one another. The biotic community also interacts with the physical environment (climate, habitats, substrata and other physical and chemical factors) to form patterns in the biosphere.

The distribution of organisms in time and space form ecological groupings in any geographical range. The *biome* concept provides a basis for evaluating the effects of climate and other abiotic factors on living organisms and also for evaluating changes brought about by man, such as cultivation and succession and survival of species after cultivation.

Living processes and the living world tend towards a balance. Because of constant changes, this balance of nature is in dynamic equilibrium.

The concept of adaptation is essential for an understanding of the distribution of organisms. Genetic mechanisms provide stability in living organisms by preserving their adaptation to the environment. Genetic adaptation (evolution) and individual adaptation (behaviour) affect the survival of individuals in the process of natural selection. Adaptation is a mode of change in time. Such change reveals itself in the diversity of species and the form and interaction of population with factors in the environment affecting population changes and fluctuations. Instances of such change are seen in the new qualities and activities which emerge among colonists and immigrants settling into new environments. A similar but sadder anthropological change is that witnessed in Indian and Aborigine peoples under the the gross changes produced in their environment by new pressures.

When we turn to history we see a similar relation between balance and change. Historical change is seen as a succession of causal shifts between states of more or less stable balance between the human forces operating over the period of change. Accordingly, the essence of history consists of the balance of human forces and its change in the course of time. In such historical phenomena as trade agreements, treaties between different countries and compromise between different groups within any nation, as in employer-worker or landlord-tenant relations or in the   function of the legal and criminal codes, we have, in essence, similar dynamic states of equilibrium to those of the biotic ecologies.

Awareness of the relation between such equilibria and changes is the mark of historical insight. Thus the progress of worker-employer relations, of salaries or of social welfare can be seen as a series of changes from one state of agreement between the persons and groups involved to another. The shift does not take place unless a change in some element in the situation such as, say, a rise in cost of living, a successful demand for higher wages or grants, or a change in working conditions, itself comes about. This change is met by appropriate action on the part of the other member elements of the state, as in lower profits, increased hours of work, more efficient production, or increased taxation, etc.

If a demand for higher wages is met but is also compensated for by demanding longer hours or more efficient work then the state of balance has been maintained. If however the demand for higher wages is met and no compensating change made in the employment conditions then a causal shift is allowed to take place, and a little piece of history has been made.

But even as we concede this link between stability and change we are no doubt troubled by the question: after admitting the dynamic nature of stability are there any properties in our experience which remain unchanged amid all the changes going on?

The answer is that man is capable of conceiving of such invariants as matter, mass, mass-energy, weight, volume, density, time, velocity, life, heredity, etc. But even these seem to have a provisional quality, for as he probes deeper into the nature of his world, the

G

thinker finds he needs to reduce the number of plainly *perceptible* qualities which remain invariant over changes in time, as when mass and energy are no longer separately conserved but become a single invariant mass-energy.

One last point may be made about the nature of stability and change. If we hold time constant and look for variation in space— as in pattern, design, shape, landscape, topography, etc., we have *structure*.

If we hold space constant and look for variation in time—as in the flow of a river, the motion of a satellite, the progress of a chemical reaction or the movement of the parts of a machine, etc., we have *process*.

Our two main problems in what immediately follows are the adolescent's awareness of the nature of dynamic stability and his ideas of change with time. We shall refer to invariance in conditions of change as and when the need arises.

ii COMPREHENSION OF THE IDEA OF DYNAMIC STABILITY

The adolescent's grasp of the idea of a stability under the action of counteractions and compensating forces and movements may be tested in many situations. The most obvious are the simple experiments of elementary physics and in their work on the growth of logical thinking. Inhelder and Piaget (op. cit.) utilized experiments on the hydraulic press, communicating vessels, the level balanced about a fulcrum, the inclined plane, and the projection of shadows. In all these cases the state of stability, be it balance, maintenance of liquid level, size of shadow, or stationary position, is maintained by an adjustment and counter-adjustment of the several forces and positions involved. By mid-adolescence the subjects in the majority began to be capable of adjusting for stability and also of explaining the systems adequately.

There are not so many nor such systematic studies of thinking about biological states of stability, as outlined in Section i, but there are indications (Perrott, 1965) that mid-adolescence marks a stage between infrequent and more regular apprehension of the dynamics of ecology. The research carried out by Rhys (op. cit.) on adolescent pupils' understanding of agricultural geography gave clear indications that the dynamics of the balance established by man with his geographical environment are not clearly perceived until 14 and upwards. This was shown particularly well in his questions on soil erosion produced by poor farming.

So far as human affairs are concerned, as seen in social and communal interrelations and in the study of history, we have growing evidence that these more subtle balances between individual and groups of people are not adequately perceived until mid to late adolescence (Wood, 1964; Peel in Burston and Thomson, 1967). In Chapter 7, research will be described on the adolescent's formation of historical concepts (De Silva, 1969) which provides further evidence to support this view. However the particular problem of social and historical equilibria could well be investigated more specifically with situations designed to reveal the difficulties met in stabilising human relations. One could also make use of biographical, literary and current affairs material.

iii WHAT ARE THE MENTAL REQUIREMENTS?

a Negating and rephrasing propositions

In order to understand and manipulate situations involving a dynamic balance of forces, the thinker should first be able to conduct his judgments in terms of propositions. Then he should be facile in the use of the negated or inverted form of proposition. This capacity showed itself very clearly in the first research on judgment (Peel, 1966) carried out in this project and reported in Chapter 2. In the test situations, 'the Pilot' and 'Jane', both evoking simple implications and propositions, a well-defined class of judgments was given in the *modus tollendo tollens* (MTT) form as opposed to the direct *modus ponendo ponens* (MPP) form (page 34).

Let us illustrate the differences between the MPP and MTT forms of the proposition of *implication* to show how a facility in negating a proposition is essential in rephrasing binary propositions. Suppose we have the following direct MPP statement *If it rains, Mrs Brown will take her umbrella*. It may be rephrased in the MTT form as follows: *If Mrs Brown is not taking her umbrella, it is not raining.*

In order to formulate the MTT form the thinker has first to be able to negate propositions and then to be aware of the effects in the binary *implication* form.

We may bring this out perhaps even clearer by adapting a standard logical lay out for each form

MPP form		MTT form	
Binary proposition	rain ⊃ * umbrella	Binary proposition	no umbrella ⊃ * no rain
Actual antecedent	rain	Actual consequence	no umbrella
Inferred consequence	umbrella	Inferred antecedent	no rain

* ⊃ = implies

Thirdly he needs to conceive of the negation of the entire binary form of implication, that is he must understand that the statement *It rains and Mrs Brown is not taking her umbrella* is a denial of the above implication.

In brief there are three requirements: *i* facility in the use of negative forms of the constituent unitary propositions, *ii* understanding of the relationship between both positive and negative forms of the antecedent and the consequence, *iii* the capacity to negate the whole binary proposition.

These requirements have been illustrated by referring to the binary proposition of *implication*, but the fundamental essential is really a grasp of the properties of the binary relations of *conjunction* and *disjunction*, particularly the formal differences between the assertion and denial of such binary forms.

Consider the following commonplace examples of assertions and denials of these binary forms. They are also symbolized in terms of standard logical nomenclature, that is by . for conjunction and v for disjunction and where the bar sign '⁻' means denial.

Conjunction

Assertion
Release the handbrake and press down the clutch   (h . c)

Denial
Either the handbrake is on or you failed to press down
the clutch $(\bar{h} \text{ v } \bar{c})$

Disjunction

Assertion
Either the road is straight or banked   **(s v b)**
Denial
The road is curved and horizontal $(\bar{s} \cdot \bar{b})$

These operations are usually understood and applied by mid-adolescents from experience of everyday action and language, even if often only implicitly, but their precise qualities and formulation can be better brought out by augmenting such experience with formal instruction.

Very often the thinker is called upon to rephrase propositions involving more complex combinations. Here is one instance:

If either the workers strike or there is an electrical blackout or Smith's fail to deliver the valves, then production will cease.

We may symbolize this as:
$(s \text{ v } b \text{ v } f) \supset c$ where the main relation is that of implication, because the factory would stop if the firm went bankrupt, was blown up, etc. We may rephrase the statement in the MTT form, in which case we have

Production will be maintained if there is no strike *and* no blackout *and* no failure in deliveries.

that is

$$\bar{c} \supset \bar{s}. \ \bar{b}. \ \bar{f}$$

With facility then in negating single and binary propositions (and the potential capacity of extending the negating operation to ternary and higher order propositions), the thinker has the mental elements for distinguishing logically between what is and is not available for manipulating the forces or movements which combine to maintain states of equilibrium. From this point in relation to actual phenomena, he needs to equate the idea of cancellation of an operation with its negation.

b Cancellation and compensation

Some unnecessary complexity and obscurity may surround our views concerning the *mental requirements* for people to cope with problems involving states of equilibria. These have arisen from Piaget's linking of the operations of thought required with the group of logical transformations on binary and higher order propositions, the so-called INRC grouping involving the identity, negation, reciprocal and correlate transformations. The matching of the psychological acts with the logical transformations comprising this group is plausible and meaningful, but the overemphasis of the phenomena in INRC terms may tend to make the psychological requirements appear to be more complicated than they are.

First we note that the situations to be dealt with are those in which two or more independent forces or movements can operate alternatively, singly or severally, to produce the state of equilibrium or a shift from it one way or another.

The steel yard-arm which can be adjusted by varying the weights or their distances from the fulcrum is an example (Inhelder and Piaget 1958, p. 164). Another, in which the whole system is in motion, would be that of an aeroplane flying in a straight line, the course of which could be altered by either cutting out an engine or turning the rudder or by a cross wind arising.

Psychologically, the thinker studying such situations has to envisage the effects of cancelling any or some of the forces operating. Let us try to see what this means by examining a few simple cases.

Suppose we have the task of maintaining the standard of salmon fishing in a river and that three independent actions affect the situation: fishing by individuals, stocking the river with young fish, control of disease. Under-fishing, restocking, control of disease would each raise the number of fish in the river, whereas over-fishing, failing to restock, absence of control against disease would lower it. The second set of changes are to be regarded as cancellations of the first set, taken by respective members. But there is more: restocking may compensate for over-fishing or loss by disease, and restricting fishing may make up for failure to restock and so on. Thus if we start with the proposition implied in under-fishing, we have its negation or cancellation in over-fishing, and an equivalent effect in either failing to restock or to control disease. These latter are negations of their respective position propositions—but not with reference to *under-fishing*. Since however they produce the same overall equilibrium or shift of it we may see that they compensate with respect to under/over-fishing. Thus the negation of any one force or action is the compensation for the others.

Such equilibria can be seen also in physical and material situations and in human affairs and political crises.

Whether or not a high jumper clears the bar may be put down, say, to two factors, the height of the bar or the quality of the take off.

The actual purchasing potential of a worker may be maintained or changed by government action on cost of living, change of number of working hours, change in wages and so on.

The mental requirements for being able to understand and manipulate situations in dynamic balance can then be fairly simply stated: the capacity to think in propositional terms, to envisage the negation of statements and rephrasing of higher order propositions in terms of their negated unitary elements in systems of equilibrium or change made up of independent forces, the power to think of these forces in action or cancelled in relation to each other, leading to the principle of compensation.

Finally there must be such an intellectual grasp of the situation as a whole that the thinker can envisage the conditions required to shift from a state of equilibrium in any way and to return to it.

The simple cancellation-compensation structure just described may not be the most effective way of comprehending situations involving two or more individual groups. Suppose we had a problem of the diplomatic relations between three countries; we could en-

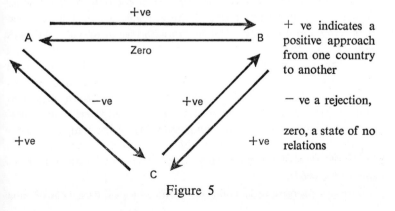

Figure 5

visage it in terms of approaches and rejections by each to the others in any sphere of political or international activity.

In order to judge and evaluate such complex states of equilibrium, which characterizes human affairs, the thinker would have to be able to manipulate and imagine changes in polyad relations. This would include a sensitivity to the psychological effects upon later diplomatic stability of, say, a change of $C \xrightarrow{+ve} A$ to zero or $-ve$, upon the $B \longrightarrow C$ relation. Such insights mark the judging of the good historian or statesman.

The elaboration of the theory of directed graphs might well provide a means for assessing the stability of such equilibria and their shifts under change.

iv THE PERSON'S AWARENESS OF THE CONDITIONS OF CHANGE

a Various manifestations

Sensitivity to sequential phenomena shows itself in several ways. First, there is the capacity to relate *cause and effect*, if need be in chain-like sequences, as in history and human studies. Then there is the individual's growing awareness of the *concept of time*, judged in terms of the cycles of changes of astronomy and the less regular non-cyclic processes revealed in biological and psychological growth, in social development and in material decay. Thirdly, as mentioned on page 97, we must be aware not only of the entities which change in time but also of those which do not, the so-called *invariant* concepts. Lastly, the person with insight into changes with time is able to predict the *directional changes* which encompass such processes as that from order to disorder and vice versa, seen in chemical reactions and changes of physical state, and in biological assimilation. There are also the changes between integrated and disintegrated structures so evident in society and human personality. Finally, there is the understanding of the template mechanism of self-producing entities which plays such an important role in the progress of bio-chemical genetics. These are means for bringing about order.

I do not propose to consider the formation of the concept of time nor of the other invariants necessary in thought. Also I do not need to say much about cause-and-effect relations. This topic has been well studied in science situations, but I would like to illustrate the differences found in cause-and-effect judgments relating to archaeological material (Thomas, 1967) calling for commonsense interpretations. An aerial photograph was presented of an archaeological site in which the buried lines of the walls and roads of a Roman town could be detected by the lighter coloured barley growing when the photograph was taken and accompanied the photograph with a short write-up about buried Roman towns. The write-up included the following paragraph:

> In a dry summer, an aerial photograph showed, plainly marked in the growing barley, the outlines of roads and the foundations of walls. These outlines were easily made out as pale streaks in the barley. The barley growing over the roads and wall foundations was lighter in colour than the barley that grew over the other parts. It was possible by using the aerial photographs, to make a street plan of the town. Later excavation showed that this plan was accurate.

The following questions were then asked of secondary school pupils:

1 How do you think the town would come to be buried?
2 Why do you think the barley growing over the roads and wall foundations was lighter in colour than the barley growing over the other areas?

The most frequently occurring answers to the first questions were bizarre, tautological, a-historical, revealing misunderstanding:

> e.g., There was an explosion—it threw sand into the ground in an avalanche of rocks—buried by attacks—a volcano.

followed by those giving a single plausible cause as a result of either natural causes or human agency:

> e.g., Flood, earthquake, decay, crumbled away, neglect, burnt or destroyed by an enemy, windblown soil, overgrown vegetation.

and finally a few consisting of a comprehensive account involving more than one imagined possibility and their joint or sequential effect:

> e.g., The ancient Britons knocked the houses down when the Romans left, virtually to nothing. Then the wind blew dust or dirt into the cracks in the brickwork and it gradually built over. Then seeds were blown over so that grass grew.

The low level answers suggest an absence of a sense of history and of material cause and effect. The wide range of explanation is most significant, for here is an apparently straightforward archaeological 'fact', which is subject to such a variety of casual interpretations.

The second question produced a similarly instructive range of answers: beginning with a-historical and perceptually dominated replies—failure to grasp the essential features of the problem—little sense of cause and effect:

> e.g., Better seed planted over the walls—sun (and rain) affected the two colours of barley differently—barley was planted by the original inhabitants—different coloured barley planted over the walls.

going on to phenomenistic explanations.

> e.g., Differences in colour due to the colour of the walls (white or lighter) or the colour of the bricks showing through—darker colour of the soil.

A single primary cause—usually lack of soil over walls or bareness of soil or obtrusion of building material—but no reference to secondary causes in differences in nutrient, water, rooting, etc.

And finishing up with imaginative connected examination of the sequence of primary and secondary causes:

> e.g., It wasn't so ripe because the roots couldn't get enough nourishment, and water from the ground because all the buildings were in the way. The other parts could get more nourishment from the ground because there was nothing in the way.

The results suggested that we may expect immature causal judgments from pupils as old as 15 years of age in relatively nontechnical situations where a multiplicity of factors operate over a long period of time.

b Order ⇌ disorder changes

I want now to explore the basis of a wide class of changes which appear to be dominated by a process of transforming random elements into ordered structure and the reverse process of going from order to disintegration. An understanding of such processes is essential for the adolescent and young adult learner in many fields of knowledge, as in the physical, biological and human sciences. Here various changes, seen in chemical reactions, energy changes, growth and decay, historical progress and economic development, form fundamental parts of the particular fields of knowledge. Some of these parts, as for instance chemical thermodynamics, often present difficulties to students yet we know surprisingly little of the psychological basis of such difficulties.

Let me first exemplify the two kinds of change simply from nontechnical sources.

i A growing plant is an ordered structure which develops, by the metabolic processes written into its seed, from the random distribution of water, air, soil chemicals and sunlight in its environment.

When the plant is pulled up or cut down it dies and rots and we see the reverse process of return from the structured entity we know as the living plant to randomly dispersed humus, salts, carbon dioxide and water.

ii When the mediaeval builders erected a castle they collected and shaped building materials which had been variously dispersed and assembled them into an integrated structure with specific functions.

Later in the course of centuries a sequence involving disuse, destruction, neglect, weathering and ageing produces the reverse change from an integrated whole to a disordered heap.

iii Human affairs show us a change from order to chaos after a catastrophic disaster like an earthquake or famine when for a short time social chaos might prevail. Such a process is shown also in the individual in the anomie or shock after severe deprivation.

The reverse process is seen in the return to order with the help and guidance of relief organizations, ordered government and individual therapy.

In order to apprehend and predict the direction of such changes the thinker must be able to conceive of the ideas of randomness, uniqueness, ordered structure, disorder, spontaneous change, promoted change, maintained cycle of events, inherent attraction.

Ideas of randomness and uniqueness may be tested and clarified by asking the pupil to experiment with a box containing an equal number of smooth black and white beads. These may be arranged so that each colour occupies one half of the box. The pupil can then be asked what will happen if they are shaken up. When the beads had been scattered at random in the box the subject may be asked if shaking will divide them back into the halves. In this way the existence of any unique mixture is related to the many others possible. Also the fact that each shake up produces a different arrangement brings out what is meant by randomness.

The idea of ordered structure and the related concept of inherent attraction between component parts are probably grasped intuitively, aesthetically and practically but they can be tested and reinforced by using a box of randomly scattered objects like paperclips, which have a characteristic shape with projections and hooks. Here shaking up will produce chains of objects hooked on to each other. Now we have rudimentary order maintained by inherent features of attraction in the component parts. This suggestion may seem trivial until one considers the template analogies of modern genetics and the function of DNA and RNA and the demands these topics make on the intellect of the young learner. Similarly the maintenance of cyclic events in astronomy and physics is seen to require forces of attraction or application of energy.

The direction of any change is determined by two factors: inherent attraction between members of the system under change and by the production of randomness. When these together result in an overall energy release in the system, whether it be physical or social, then the change will take place. Let us consider two examples. Nitro-glycerine is such an effective explosive, first, because in its structure is harnessed enormous energy which is released when it disintegrates (into randomness) and, second, because the simple chemical products of the change include nitrogen, water, and carbon dioxide, all of which are highly stable, that is, whose parts have strong inherent attraction. Next, suppose we think of a group of strangers trapped together in a lift for a long time. When they are released there will be a strong tendency for dispersal (to randomness). This change would be stronger, say, if two of the strangers found a mutual interest and pleasure in each other and decided to meet in future (inherent attraction between members of a unit).

In the above instances inherent attraction of parts and production of randomness augment each other to produce the changes outlined. This may not always be so, for we may have in fact three possible outcomes in any order $\rightleftharpoons$ randomness change. We may have:

	new units made of parts having	*amount of randomness*
1	stronger inherent attraction (+)	greater (+)
2	„ „ „ (+)	smaller (−)
3	weaker „ „ (−)	greater (+)

We suggest that the direction change will be determined by the overall balance of released energy. This being so, in case 2 the inherent attraction forces must exceed the loss of randomness and, in case 3, the weaker bonded units must be more than compensated for by the rise in amount of randomness.

A commonplace instance of 2 would be seen when two people marry successfully. Here the strongly bonded union more than compensates for the loss of freedom for them as individuals (loss of randomness). Britain's mooted entry into the Common Market can be seen as another instance. As to case 3, we can exemplify this by the practice of incarcerating wrong-doers in prisons. As inmates of a prison they manifest little inherent mutual attraction, and have in fact to be held together by prison walls. However society gains as a whole in freedom from crime. In this sense there is greater randomness in the whole system.

Some of the passage material used in the investigations already described test the germs of these ideas about change, particularly where questions are asked about possible future action as in some of the material devised by Rhys (op. cit.). However more needs to be done to assess this sensitivity to the conditions making for change and the judgment technique would seem to have much to offer.

The reader acquainted with chemistry and physics will no doubt recognize that randomness is what the scientists call entropy. To grasp this concept calls for thinking about the *presence* of randomness rather than the *absence* of order. The former is a more sophisticated concept and may well appear only in later adolescence as do other inversions like the conservation of momentum (Inhelder and Piaget, 1958, p. 123). Although the idea of entropy started in the physical sciences it has been extended to the social and linguistic sciences to account for random base states from which to develop hypotheses in these fields. Since the concepts of directional change, inherent attraction of parts and randomness or entropy are so important I have attempted, in an appendix to the chapter, to provide a non-mathematical exposition of the chemist's views about them.

c Summing up

Much of this section has been speculative and suggestive of future investigation into a mode of thinking very important in higher learning.

In comprehending order $\rightleftharpoons$ disorder changes the thinker has to envisage two tendencies, the formation or breaking up of groups bound together by inherent forces and of the tendency for spontaneous change to lead to greater randomness, the reverse change requiring energy to be put into the system. Also he has to grasp the idea of presence of randomness rather than absence of order.

We have little psychological evidence of the adolescent's power to form and utilize these sequential notions, although research on children's ideas of change bears on the problem. What we need are test situations where we can present ordered material—carry out the equivalent of a spontaneous change and ask for predictions of the outcome. We could use material from a wide field including human affairs. Some similarity between social reactions and the chemical reaction may be seen. First, as to strong inherent bonding releasing social energy we may note the lack of social strain brought about by, say, a learned society whose members are bound by common interests, and the strain on society's energies, in keeping in a gaol a group of prisoners who have no common interest in being held together. The former case leaves more social energy available for other things; the latter requires social energy to maintain it. As to the idea of social entropy, one might perceive it in the result of a sudden cessation of an over-ordered community as in a communist or fascist state. There would be an immediate spontaneous rise of independent action having a chaotic quality. The same is true after a war or when a small overruled community such as a school or home breaks up.

We have noted that in order to bring order from randomness some energizing principle is necessary and the thinker has to be aware of this requirement in a full understanding of the complete two-way possibility. Reorganizing society and self-replication of biochemicals by template action (Clowes, 1967, Chap. 10, Penrose, 1958) are instances of the reverse process of producing order from randomness.

Finally we may note the profound significance in our total environment, material, social and personal, of the order $\rightleftharpoons$ disorder changes in time. We have seen that this mechanism itself calls for several important concepts and for a co-ordinate interaction of two basic processes, bonding by inherent forces between individuals and the spontaneous appearance of randomness. We know little as to how adolescents acquire these ideas, but from what we have learned about other aspects of their judgments, their middle years will be important. For instance, much of the discussion voiced by older adolescents about the nature of freedom and authority implies these two basic concepts. Almost everything needs to be done to investigate how they develop.

V APPENDIX—A CHEMICAL DIVERSION

The chemist begins by asking a question: Why do chemical reactions occur?

This question can be answered in non-algebraic terms (Sanderson, 1964) but it requires an understanding of the few fundamental ideas of spontaneous reaction, order, randomness, amount of disorder, force of attraction and energy absorption and emission.

A *spontaneous* chemical reaction is one having the potential to proceed without the assistance of an external agency. We judge the progress of a reaction by comparing its final with its initial state, that is, the products with the original reactants. As Sanderson writes, 'the *direction* of spontaneity remains the most important property of a chemical reaction'.

Randomness is best imagined if we think of all the constituent *atoms* making up the molecules of the reactants and the products being all separated and mixed up freely moving about in a gaseous state. Now although the reaction is going from reactants to products, we may see it in terms of the more likely or probable recombination of the randomly moving free atoms, to give either reactant molecules or product molecules. The chemists assume that, other things being equal, the direction of the spontaneous change (to reactants or products) will be that which 'involves least departure from the original randomness'. That is, the direction of spontaneous change will be from reactants to products, if the latter constitute a more *random* state.

The other condition is that where there are strong inherent *forces of attraction* between certain atoms and molecules making for stable bonds, then the direction of the spontaneous reaction will be such as to form such products. Overall a reaction tends 'to occur spontaneously in the direction of stronger bonds and less organized array', to quote Sanderson.

Fortunately, we do not need to go into chemical thermodynamics beyond remarking that the above statement implies that the free energy content of the system is diminished in a spontaneous change, the diminution showing itself as a discharge of energy as heat, light, etc. The diminution may be achieved by the two tendencies working together in the following alternative ways:

a Formation of stronger bonds and greater randomness,

b Formation of stronger bonds and less randomness (but the randomness is not so low as to absorb the energy released by the formation of the stronger bonds),

c Formation of weaker bonds and greater randomness (greater randomness must more than compensate for the energy absorbed into the system to form weaker bonded chemicals).

The randomness is called *entropy* and where 'these two influences of bond strength and entropy are in conflict, the final outcome will depend on their relative contributions in the reaction' (Sanderson). (See modes b and c above.)

Overall a spontaneous reaction generates energy and randomness and the reverse process of a non-spontaneous reaction requires energy and leads to lowering of entropy.

CHAPTER SIX

Promoting Mature Judgment

i SENSITIVITY OF THE ACT OF JUDGING

At several places in the discussion of investigations into the maturity of adolescent judgment we have come across indications that the level of judgment may be quite susceptible to cultural and educational influences. In the very first preliminary trials of the material it was found that a group of boys from markedly superior socio-economic backgrounds made more mature reasoned judgments than boys from homes at lower socio-economic levels. This greater maturity was clearly distinguished even when the groups of pupils were matched for verbal reasoning by customary traditional tests. This result was later confirmed (Chapter 3, Section ii b) by the discovery of a significant correlation between socio-economic level and maturity of judgment. On the educational side we reported

(Chapter 3, Section iv b) that a multiple choice form of response, from an array including answers at all levels of maturity, leads to more mature judgments than the open ended form of question produced. Here the information provided in the multiple choice form seems to act as an instruction device.

On the other hand it appears that it is not enough merely to provide more information in the test passage material (Chapter 3, Section iii a). This might mean that there is an element of 'readiness' involved in the act of judgment and that a knowledge of such readiness would have to be taken into consideration if programmes of instruction were to be contemplated. But this would not deny that a more positive programme of teaching geared to the thinker's level of development may be fruitful, in which the several facets and stages of the act of judging are brought to his awareness.

ii WHAT IS GENERAL IN MAKING SPECIFIC JUDGMENTS

Any scheme of tuition or graded experience calculated to produce better insights into the act of judging must proceed from what we have discovered about the stages and facets of the process.

The major empirical finding has been the distinction in a wide range of test situations between the three levels of judgment, labelled *restricted*, *circumstantial* and *comprehensive-imaginative*. Although during and after adolescence we would expect only a small minority of restricted judgments, these are in fact prevalent enough to compel us to include provision for them in any teaching programme. However, the main distinction is between the partial, circumstantial answers and the more imaginative and circumspect replies. Teaching must be directed towards enabling the thinkers to cross this bridge. There is more than a hint that a readiness element is present in this problem, since in the normal setting of Western education the ages of 13–14 come up again and again as times of transition from circumstantial to circumspect judgment.

Imaginative circumspect judgments entail several elements. First there is the power to invoke through the imagination possible explanations or hypotheses. These also have to be formulated and made explicit. Then there is the double-faceted act of evaluation of these possibilities entailing the selection of the most appropriate and elimination of the least desirable in relation to the general features of the problem.

This act of intellectual evaluation calls for deductive thinking and may invoke the power of sustained argument. Specific ingredients of such arguing are:

a detection of inconsistencies and partialities
b ability to examine a situation formally and structurally, as opposed to circumstantially and merely contentwise
c the capacity to relate the test-material to the offered hypothesis
d a capacity to reason propositionally
e a mastery of language in relation to reason.

Finally, there is the more subtle susceptibility of the thinker to the properties of physical and social environments in constant change. This entails sensitivity of the judger to problems of equilibrium and change. Our researches have suggested at various points that the capacity to deal with opposing and compensating forces and trends is not marked normally in Western schools until 14+. Again the question of readiness is raised. We have a little evidence that the dynamics of change from an organized ecological state to a disorganized one, and vice versa, are also not appreciated until even later.

These qualities, at least, general to a wide range of problem situations calling for judgment, must be kept in mind in preparing for any course of instruction on making judgments.

ii SOME RELEVANT RESEARCH ON IMPROVING THE
   QUALITY OF THINKING

I make no attempt to survey the vast field of research on transfer of training which might at some points bear on the topic of training judgment. I want, however, to outline two or three pieces of research, characterized by the same basic spirit of attack on problems of thinking which appear to mark the research described in this monograph on adolescent judgment.

The first is that conducted by Suchman (1961, 1964). He investigated classroom conditions necessary to stimulate and sustain the inquiring mind in children. He was disturbed by the degree to which school pupils leaned on the intellectual authority of their teachers, with a growing atrophy of their own spirit of inquiry. He used films of simple phenomena in physics, with which the children were not familiar and which were discrepant with their previous experience—as in the bimetal blade which bends differently as it is turned over in a flame. The pupils were allowed to ask questions which could be answered only by 'yes' and 'no'. Such questions in fact embody the statement of hypotheses which are tested when the question is put and the answer received, and on the basis of the answers the pupils 'build better theories which they test themselves'.

These learning-to-think sessions had the following features:

  i The child is provided with a problem, made of elements discrepant to the existing conceptual systems of the child (as in the film showing the dicerent bending of a bimetallic blade), which acts as a *focus* for his attention.

 ii Freedom to pursue any line of inquiry the child wishes to follow. This freedom is both external,

  to reach out for desired data and information and to acquire it at any rate in any sequence the child wishes

and consequently is also internal, by which they

  make decisions and try to satisfy their own cognitive needs by gathering the kinds of information they want. They also exercise freedom in trying out ideas.

iii An informative response from the teacher when the child probes forward.

Here is an excerpt from a session on the film of the bimetallic blade:

Steve:	Could you have done it without heating it once?
Examiner:	Yes.
Steve:	Could you keep on heating this and the knife would keep bending?
Examiner:	Yes.
Steve:	Would it ever break from going up and down?
Examiner:	No, not from that—not from going up and down.
Steve:	Did the water have anything to do with it bending the second time?
Examiner:	Find out.
Steve:	If you had put this thing over a cold vent of air would the things have gone back down?
Examiner:	Yes.

Steve: Was the water in the thing cold?

Each session is tape-recorded and there follows a playback and discussion.

The effects of this 'inquiry training' appear to transfer to other fields, as in biology and economics. Suchman was doing more than teaching his pupils elementary physics—he was teaching them to think. He is not suggesting that inquiry or discovery should replace good didactic exposition. As he says,

> If a child had to discover every new relationship for himself, a great deal of time and energy would be wasted. Gifted children in particular are capable of acquiring elaborate conceptual systems through explanations and demonstrations. But more basic than the attainment of concepts is the ability to inquire and discover these autonomously.

Suchman limited himself to simple science problems but Crutchfield and Covington (1963) used more general material calculated to interest children in late childhood and early adolescence. Their objective was to train 'for a generalized problem-solving skill' and for this reason did not limit themselves to specific curricular content.

They, therefore, avoided particular school material and drew their lessons from a selection of puzzles and mysteries such as the theft of a museum object and odd happenings in an empty house. Each lesson was built around a single mystery, and the characters, two children and their uncle, by their actions and discourse provided more clues and information so that the learner was finally led to find a solution himself. At various points in each lesson the learner himself was challenged so that he had to make various problem-solving responses.

Each lesson was part of a continuous theme and required forty-five minutes. The children were then given test problems, including the Duncker X-ray problem. It was found that the experimental group did better. For example, out of ninety-eight children taking the learning problem, 35 per cent solved the X-ray problem whereas, among a matched control of ninety-seven children not so instructed, only 13 per cent were able to solve the problem.

Later, Biran (1968) constructed a learning programme on transpiration, to teach from a particular example how to design experiments to test hypotheses, and how to draw conclusions from data.

In the part on experimental design, an experimental strategy is suggested to the learner in general terms. He then applies it to the phenomenon under study, and is led to suggest an appropriate experiment and predict possible outcomes. In the part where conclusions are drawn, the learner examines the validity of a hypothesis put forward in the programme to explain unexpected results.

Preliminary results indicated that the programme achieved its purpose.

In these investigations and attempts to teach the pupil to think, to solve problems and to imagine and evaluate hypotheses, the individual is placed in a position where he has to state the problem and offer his solution. At the same time the teaching programme provides him with opportunities for checking his progress.

The essence of the process is that of a free exchange of ideas and material between pupil and teacher with an optimum load of responsibility being placed on the thinker for solving his own problems.

iv RAISING THE LEVEL OF JUDGMENT BY TEACHING

a **By traditional methods of teaching**

A study of the effect of traditional instruction in thinking upon the maturity of pupils' judgments was carried out by Anderson (op. cit.). The results were compressed in Table XVII of Chapter 3 (p. 59) in order to bring out the influence of the multiple choice form of response. The findings however have not been discussed primarily with reference to the effect of the teaching.

In all, Anderson examined the influence of age, ability, answer form and instruction on making judgments. He had eight groups of eight pupils who received instruction in thinking and shared discussion on its essentials and eight other groups who had no such experience. Three of the eight passages with their two forms of questions are given in Appendix 4 (p. 165).

The course of instruction on making judgments

The rationale of the course of four topics in judgment was based on teaching the pupils first how to recognize inconsistencies, incompatabilities, irrelevances, and partialities. In terms of the notation of symbolic logic, the instruction was often concerned with class-relation, class membership, and overlapping classes. Here are instances of material discussed in the first topic.

	Yes	No
Can you be obedient and disobedient at the same time to the same person?	—	—
Can you be obedient and clumsy at the same time?	—	—
If you are judging a girl's dancing does it matter whether she can cook?	—	—
If you are deciding whether to make friends with a girl does it matter whether she is kind?	—	—
If you are judging a man's character does it matter what nationality he is?	—	—
Magazines can be black-and-white or coloured and dull or interesting	—	—
Can a dull magazine be interesting?	—	—
Can an interesting magazine be black-and-white?	—	—
Can a coloured magazine be dull?	—	—

The second topic was mainly concerned with reasoning from propositional statements to arrive at conditions under which statements might be true, false or inconclusive.

	True	False	Maybe
It is always dangerous to drive fast	—	—	—
It is sometimes dangerous to drive fast	—	—	—
It is never dangerous to drive slow	—	—	—

Others deal with looking for relevant reasons, since our results have repeatedly shown that irrelevance of information is often a stumbling block to sustained reasoning.

If a man causes an accident you should consider whether he
was   (rich   clever   old   careless)

Anderson was also concerned with the capacity to evoke reasons and to evaluate them, as in the following instance:

Yesterday, while it was raining I walked along dry pavements.

	Yes	No
Is this what you would normally expect?	—	—
Although this doesn't happen normally, could there be a sensible reason for saying this?	—	—

Which of these reasons do you consider sensible?

a I was walking very quickly
b I was walking along the main shopping street
c I was using my umbrella
d I travelled by bus
e it was only a shower

The third topic was concerned with teaching the pupils the pitfalls of implication and with propositions involving the quantifiers *all* and *some*.

Doctors have discovered that people who have a disease called scurvy have swollen gums and painful sores. You are not likely to catch this if you have plenty of fresh fruit and vegetables in your diet.

	Yes	No	Can't Say
a Jane has scurvy. Are her gums swollen?	—	—	—
b John has swollen gums. Has he got scurvy?	—	—	—
c Jill's gums are not swollen but she has several painful sores. She likes apples. Has she got scurvy?	—	—	—
d In the old days of sailing ships, sailors lived for months on a very salt diet with no fresh food. Were they likely to get scurvy?	—	—	—
e Can you be ill through eating too much fruit?	—	—	—
f A man has sailed round the world on his own and apart from a few accidents has been healthy all the time. Did he carry fresh food with him?	—	—	—

and then moved on to the problem of relevance in argument.

Newspapers and magazines nowadays contain many bright, amusing, or interesting advertisements. Which of these statements tells you the main purpose of an advertisement?

a Advertisements tell you everything about a product.
b Advertisements tell you the whole truth.
c Advertisements always lie.

d Advertisements are intended to make you want to buy a product.

e Advertisements are put in to make the magazine pretty.

The fourth topic closes with a very full discussion of a judgment problem of the type used in the test situations.

Statement: In the Middle Ages most men lived all their lives without being able to read. They built beautiful cathedrals but did not know many of the ordinary, everyday things which every child of twelve knows nowadays. Every age builds upon the knowledge of those who went before. *Question*: Were the people of the Middle Ages clever or stupid? How do you know?

The teaching questions included the following:

a Does it say that all men of the Middle Ages were unable to read?

b Are you always clever because you can read?

c Is a person who cannot read always stupid?

d Are all people clever nowadays?

e Why is it that many ordinary modern children of twelve know more about some things than very clever people of the past?

f Is the passage really about beautiful things or about cleverness?

g If there are two main ideas and one is more important than the other, which one would your answer be about mainly?

h How do you decide the best answer to any question or how do you set about judging something?

The results

The answers to the tests were graded on the three-point scale described in Chapter 3 but out of the total number of responses of 1024, there were only sixteen restricted *a* responses. Anderson therefore dichotomized the responses into those not exceeding *b* (including the sixteen *a* responses) and mature *c* responses. This meant that the data could be adequately condensed and organized in terms of the frequencies of mature *c* responses as given in Table XXIV and set out in the graphical form which follows it.

Table XXIV Percentage increases in imaginative responses due to tuition

		Instructed I	Uninstructed U	(I - U)	% increase
Younger	abler — M/C	52	44	8	18·2
	abler — free	46	15	31	206·7
	less able — M/C	41	28	13	46·4
	less able — free	24	6	18	300·0
Older	abler — M/C	55	53	2	3·8
	abler — free	56	28	28	100·0
	less able — M/C	47	40	7	17·5
	less able — free	38	21	17	81·0

These results bring out very clearly the extent of the influence of the teaching on the maturity of judgment. It is relatively more effective with the free responses, the educative effect of the multiple-choice response being so marked as to leave less room for further improvement by the formal teaching given on the four topics. It is also interesting how the abler streams (1A and 3A) respond more readily to the course of lessons on thinking.

The relative effect of the teaching can be portrayed by calculating the percentage increase in the number of c responses obtained after instruction. This merely involves calculating the term $\dfrac{100(I - U)}{U}$, where U is the number of c responses from the uninstructed groups and I is the number from the instructed groups. These have been calculated in the last two columns of Table XXIV.

Here we see the relative effectiveness of the teaching programme when the learner is called to make a free response—but we note still the absolute superiority of teaching combined with multiple-choice answering.

The results set out in Table XXIV may be put in graphical form as follows, in order to illustrate these observations:

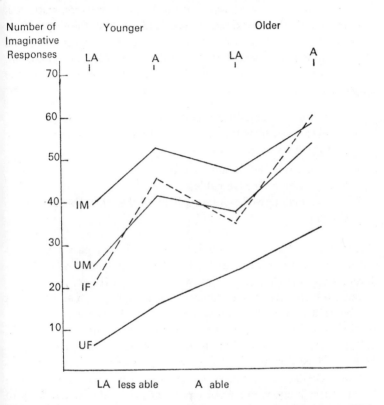

Instructed groups: Free responses (IF) Uninstructed: Free responses (UF)
Instructed groups: Multiple choice (IM) Uninstructed groups: Multiple choice (UM)

By dividing his post-test situations into two halves separated by a five week interval, Anderson was also able to demonstrate that the instruction had a more long-term effect than the multiple-choice form of response.

b By programmed techniques

An interesting possibility arises (Peel, July 1967) of using the actual responses obtained in investigations of persons' judgments, as described in Chapter 2, as a means of teaching individuals how to judge. The idea suggested was that the range of answers, restricted, circumstantial and imaginative, obtained in 'the Pilot' problem, might well be utilized to construct a branching programme based on this problem and aimed at raising the general level of judgment. Thus in the first frame one might present the anecdote and the question:

> Was the pilot a careful airman? and then ask the learner to select his answer from the following actual responses, representing all three levels of judgment
>
> 1 Yes, the cable should not have been there,
> 2 No, because he hit the cable,
> 3 Yes, he may have flown into a bank of mist that obscured his vision.

According to the learner's choice one could then pass him on to other frames which must at least include a judgment at as low a level as the one chosen by him in the previous frame.

Such a technique would have certain advantages. The responses in the frames would be chosen from actual responses made by adolescents. The branching technique would enable one to have a full discussion of the limitations of certain judgments. This discussion could be directed finally to promoting general judgment.

Gray (1970), an experienced programmer and user of programmed techniques in school work, undertook the first inquiry to find out whether these ideas were feasible. He produced five branching programmed texts for training different aspects of judging, each requiring up to forty minutes for completion. To quote Gray:

> The approach, through the medium of the verbal logic of a branching programme was:
>
> a to indulge the child's current level of thinking on the particular topic long enough for him to become aware of his limitations;
> b to lead the child deliberately into the next higher level of thinking by challenge, argument, the production of further information, and so on;

c to encourage, at the hypothetico-deductive stage, a consideration of all possibilities and the subsequent discarding
   of those unwanted;
d to encourage divergent thinking—the production of many
   ideas—yet also to provide opportunities for the convergent
   thinking involved in carrying an argument to a conclusion.

Three of the programmes were based on problems already discussed:

Pilot problem (Chapter 2, p. 32; see also Appendix 5)
Four-minute miler problem (Chapter 4, p. 71)
Canadian Prairies problem (Rhys op. cit.)

One was based on Duncker's Radiation problem (1945), the responses to which were given by him at some length. The fifth programme was based on the missing coins problem of Covington and
Crutchfield (1965).

Randomly selected experimental and control groups of secondary
school pupils were chosen and the experimental groups went
through the five branching programmes at a rate of one per day for
five consecutive days.

Both groups then took a post-test of six thinking problems. Three
were judgment problems: Jane (Peel, 1966), New Roads (Anderson, op. cit.) and the puzzle of the Missing Package (Covington and
Crutchfield, op. cit.). The remaining items consisted of two problem solving situations: the ropes problem (Duncker, 1945) and the
similar pit problem, and finally the divergent thinking test: Unusual Uses (Minnesota Tests of creative thinking and writing).

Gray found that those adolescents taking the course of five programmes on how to think and judge obtained significantly higher
scores on the Jane, New Roads and Lost Package tests. However
there was no significant difference between the performance of experimental and control groups on the Ropes, Pit and Unusual Uses
tests.

His programmes appeared to be effective in promoting mature
judgment. He also concluded that analysis of judgment may exist
independently alongside work on divergent thinking and problem
solving.

A third research was directly concerned with the effect of instruction in relevant historical concepts upon the maturity of historical

judgments (1967). Stones had earlier demonstrated (1965) that the broad (three-category) scheme of analysing judgments (Chapter 2) applied substantially to historical material. She improved the test material by taking an area of history not widely read by English Secondary Schools. This was the history of the growth of the American transcontinental railway systems from 1830 to 1900. (See Appendix 6 for an example of this test material.)

She was able to refine the basic three-point scale of grading the pupils' judgment to form six categories which were, beginning with the lowest:

Grade 1: restricted;

Grade 2: circumstantial-direct;

Grade 3: Circumstantial—use of conditional mood—sometimes inversion given;

Grade 4: causal links;

Grade 5: causal chaining;

Grade 6: hypothetical deductive reasoning.

Her subjects, adolescent secondary school pupils from a wide range of ability, were divided randomly into two groups. The experimental group followed the linear programme of instruction of sixty-two frames on concepts underlying the subsequent history material used in the judgment tests. These concepts included trade, transport, goods, imports, exports, market, etc. The control group received a list of the definitions of the same concepts. Both groups then read the three passages of history and wrote down their responses to the three questions on each passage. The responses were then scored on the six-point qualitative scale reflecting the level of reasoning. The sum total for the nine questions was then used as a measure of the pupils' ability to make judgments about the historical material used.

The group receiving the programmed instruction achieved significantly higher scores on the judgment tests. The improvement was most marked among pupils of higher intelligence and lower verbal fluency. Those of lower intelligence and fluency show an increase in their ability to understand the questions and the passages of history but are still unable to progress to the higher levels of explanatory thinking in their written responses to the questions.

It will be seen that the significant differences attributable to fluency and intelligence, which were in fact stronger even than those due to instructions, confirm results set out in Chapter 3.

These differences due to the programmed instruction in the economic concepts support the findings on the effects of teaching general judgment and hold out hope for possible further work in geography, current affairs and literary criticisms.

CHAPTER SEVEN

Concept Formation During and After Adolescence

i WHY WE NEED TO STUDY CONCEPT FORMATION

In the foregoing chapters we have discussed in some detail the capacity of the adolescent to make judgments and in so doing have completed the major purpose of this book. At various points, however, particularly in the first and second chapters, the role of concepts in the explanation of here and now events has been stressed. As we have not examined the specific features of concept formation during the adolescent years it seems desirable to have at least some subordinate study of them to complete our account of the intellectual life of the adolescent.

Such an ancillary section on concept formation is justified if

a concepts are important principles of explanation, accounting for new phenomena under study;

b there are features of concept formation which are peculiar to adolescence and early adulthood.

The first condition has been apparent at many points in the text for the most mature imaginative judgments always imply the invocation of more general or higher level ideas. It is the absence of such invocation which characterizes circumstantial thought.

As to the second condition, I hope to convince the reader that there are special features of adolescent concept formation which warrant comment and investigation.

ii WHAT TO SELECT

Our discussion will be confined to the growth of adolescent conceptual thinking and we shall limit ourselves to those topics which seem to bear on the growth of judgment during adolescence.

Of the wealth of empirical studies and writing on the problem of concept formation relatively little has been done on the adolescent. Often the material used in these experiments on concept learning is specific and even very artificial, being limited frequently to conjunctive concepts whose attributes are shapes, colours, sizes and numbers. These inevitably restrict the adult subject's activity to attainment of the trick concept devised by the experimenter. The subject is not put in a position of having to search for attributes to define his concepts as is often required of him in coming to terms with the relational concepts of human knowledge, as for instance in dealing with the data: *aggression, unilateralism, exploitation* which in many people's minds would lead to the more general concept of *inhumanity*. The adolescent has at his disposal criteria, long learned, such as colour, shape and size, by which to group concrete experiences but he may have no such ready-made abstractions for the more complex phenomena of higher human learning. The data of spectroscopy, crystallography, astronomy, genetics, the humanities and linguistics are variously complex, abstract, perhaps deceptively simple and may also have to be mediated by language.

I

We could well put the student in the position of Mendel (Clowes 1967, pp. 28–32; Taton, 1962, pp. 127–8), when confronted with the results of his long series of experiments on the cultivation and cross-fertilization of different kinds of peas, such as red-flowered and white-flowered, or smooth and wrinkled. For example, in one experiment he cross-fertilized red- and white-flowered peas and obtained a first generation wholly of red-flowered products. He then produced a second generation of peas from these entirely red-flowered peas and obtained 705 red-flowered peas and 224 white-flowered peas.

Viewing this as a problem in concept formation, we may first note the deceptive simplicity of the data. The difficulty is to know where to start, and in this type of genetic problem the tasks prove almost impossible to carry out unless there is some previous guidance in the thinking about the numbers of different kinds of offspring.

The concepts eventually evolved include: separate distinct units of traits in each parent, their transmission to the offspring by chance, atomistic inheritance, dominance-recessiveness of traits. These concepts are subsumed in the wider concept of heredity.

Thus the student and older pupil, like the young child in front of an array of simple patterns and colours, may often in his more sophisticated study of advanced enquiry and explanation find himself in the position of having to devise his own attributes or criteria of action in order to solve his problems.

We need therefore to consider how far adolescents and adults experience difficulties in forming classes and relations and the concepts based on them.

Next we have the phenomenon that a concept has three parts of psychological and educational significance: the array or class of instances, the underlying rule which defines the concept, and the name used to communicate the concept. The overt statement of the defining rule often presents difficulties even when the array is recognized. I shall discuss research on the development of capacity to cope with these aspects.

Lastly we note the nearly related feature of mature thought, that its coinage in all fields consists of abstractions. In discussions of scientific results and theories and in the evaluations of human affairs and creations the thinker has to be expert in manipulating the *-ions* and *-isms*. There may be a distinction between judging that *X was an aggressor* and expressing the opinion that *aggression is a feature of Imperialism*. Since older adolescents enjoy discussion of ideas and are expected to produce connected discourse about them, I shall consider the relationship between abstraction and generalization and produce empirical evidence on the capacity of the adolescent and adult to abstract.

iii CLASSIFICATION AND CONCEPT FORMATION

We may easily demonstrate that adolescents have some difficulties, which we normally associate with childhood, in the act of classifying, particularly if the material is verbal. If for instance they are asked to identify subordinate or superordinate classes by their names among lists of terms which include partially associated entities and meaningful, contiguous and similar but illogically connected elements, the majority are not likely in early adolescence to form inclusive classes. Even by 15 years of age a sizeable minority seem still not able to recognize the inclusions

| particular object | < | class of objects | < | superordinate class of objects |

in such circumstances.

Here are the results of an investigation carried out with two groups of adolescents of average ability and of mean ages 12 + and 16 +, compared with a group of adults of superior ability.

The test situation was as follows:

This is a test of your understanding of words and phrases. Each test consists of two rows of words or phrases. In the first row there are three words or phrases which are related to each other in a certain way. You are to discover this relationship and then to use it as a guide for completing the second row. This you do by underlining what you think is the correct word or phrase wherever there is a column of five alternatives.

Here is an example which is done for you:

Robin Hood	outlaw	man
daisy	flower	horticulture
		petal
		bush
		plant
		bouquet

Now do these two by first examining the three parts of the first row to find how they are related and then picking the word or phrase in the column of the second row which most nearly completes the same relationship as in the first row.

1 Ford   car   vehicle
  Harrogate   town   Yorkshire
                                      city
                                      population centre
                                      local government
                                      health resort

2 Westminster Abbey church   building
  Bobby Charlton   footballer   Manchester United player
                                      English International
                                      baldheaded man
                                      sportsman
                                      brother of Jackie Charlton

The results are given in Table XXV where the correct response, the superordinate class name, has been italicized. The percentage of other responses is given in the last row against each test item. The variously partial, contiguous, associated but logically irrelevant answers are seen against the four alternatives in the mulitple choice. At least Bobby Charlton's bald head is seen as an irrelevance!

Concept formation has its roots in the logical similarities and differences between the members of any array of material. But what the immature thinker takes as similarities may not be logically based. Also in the above 3-step situation the wrong response gives evidence of a shift of criteria by which to judge similarity. This is a feature frequently noted in research on concept formation (Werner and Kaplan, 1950; Bruner et al 1966).

These researches all show that the ability to form groups on the basis of logically abstracted criteria has to be learned and that even adolescents, if the test is verbal, tend to make use of criteria available to them and that these may be of a thematic or associational kind. Furthermore often the nature of the criterion can change but the thinker still manages to assimilate the changes in his abstractions.

Table XXV Frequency of responses

	1st year 12+	5th year 16+	Adults
Yorkshire	11	7	2
city	13	10	—
population centre	6	9	28
local government	1	2	—
health resort	1	2	2
Total other responses	26	21	4
% other responses	81·3	70·0	12·5
Manchester United player	11	4	1
English International	1	4	—
baldheaded man	—	—	—
sportsman	15	22	31
brother of Jackie Charlton	4	—	—
Total other responses	16	8	1
% other responses	51·6	26·7	3·1

When however an individual can group an array logically by picking out those members having a certain property, combination of properties, or relationships his ability to deal with the array in this way would lead us to expect him to recognize the non-membership class. More generally he could form the logical inclusions and exclusions, hierarchies and cross-groupings implied in the logic of classes.

1 Selecting the criteria (or attributes) on which the act of grouping is based;
2 The awareness of the formal properties of the act of grouping.

Although we have demonstrated above with verbal material as Korstvedt *et al* (1954) did with non-verbal sorting tests, that the younger average adolescent has some trouble in classifying, in general adolescents possess an awareness of the formal properties of classification.

These aspects of logical classification are instances of two more fundamental and general types of experience and organizing action carried out by humans on their world. First there are the acts of grouping, counting, measuring and any other way of organizing our experiences and environment. Then there are the properties of these acts which lead eventually to logic, algebra, geometry and trigonometry. They give us the differences between the empirical and practical sciences and the formal sciences of grammar, logic and mathematics. We expect adolescents to operate successfully in these fields.

iv RELATIONAL CONCEPTS

By far the most extensive type of concept used in the sciences and humanities is the relational concept. It embodies a relationship between different features in each instance, as shown in the concept triangle within a circle and in other topological ideas. Most concepts of geometry are relational as in the idea of the tangent, gradient, interior angle and circle and so are many of those science like velocity, momentum, density, chemical reaction, chemical bond, heat, growth, digestion and environment. On the humanities side, we have the relational concepts of law, employee, aristocracy, rain shadow, harmony, rhythm, poetry, morality, justice, authority, government and debate.

The implications of this state of affairs is clear for students of adolescent thinking. We must know more about how pupils and students arrive at relational concepts, since so much of higher learning is based on them.

When we turn first to psychological investigations, using devised relational concepts, we find that there are lamentably few devoted to the relational thinking of adolescents and students. With the exception of the classical study by Smoke (1932) and an attempt by Cronbach and Azuma (1961) to investigate students' powers to deal with difficult relational concepts in co-ordinate geometry, there have been few penetrative psychological pieces of research on relational thinking. Some years ago I used relational combinations of shapes to test practical intelligence in secondary school pupils and architecture and engineering students. Here is one item:

Figure 7

Mark with a cross the wrong part
of the design

The tests revealed a wide range of capacity to solve relational
problems.

As regards studies of actual relational concepts, constructed to
account for man's natural environment, we have much more
evidence about the growth of such concepts as space, distance,
time, speed and causality. Much of this information is due to the
monumental work of Piaget, Inhelder and their associates on the
child's awareness of physical reality (1955) and the growth of
logical thinking in adolescence (1962). But it must be re-emphasized
that we know little about the adolescent formation of the more
complex relational concepts called for in human knowledge.

V ADOLESCENT AND ADULT CONCEPT FORMATION

The light of mature reason does not suddenly shed its clarity upon
the young adolescent as by a magic wand: the growth from childhood to late adolescence is continuous. How regular we do not
know, but according to the difficulty, abstractness and complexity
of the ideas involved we may expect to find in older people some
similar manifestations of incomplete conceptual processes.

For example, some of the child's logically restricted transduc-
tions are repeated by what looks superficially like the same thing
in adults. Thus we have the story of the customs officer who had
to decide whether copies of a sociological questionnaire were
subject to duty. He is said to have argued as follows: a question-

naire is a puzzle, a puzzle is a toy, a toy is taxable, therefore the questionnaire is taxable.

Indeed propagandists and other folk whose aim is to persuade the public against their reason may well seek to inculcate such tendencies for their own persuasive purposes by deliberately mentioning a man's private weaknesses or strengths to create a misleading picture of his public potentialities.

Let me pull together certain ideas hinted at so far. In the formation of new concepts of value in higher learning the following operations may be involved:

   i The thinker has to discover new attributes often of a non-perceptual mediated kind.

   ii Very often the concepts involve relations as opposed to attributes, and the thinker has to look for common relationships. This requirement is well illustrated in the new physics course where pupils are encouraged to form the relational concept of force from several instances of sources of force.

   iii Having once made explicit the criteria of action involved in grouping entities embodying a particular concept, the thinker has to become cognizant of the formal properties of these criteria, for instance in the case of the concept of force, he is able to manipulate deductively equations expressing the relationship.

   iv More rarely and in specific areas of science the conceptualization of advanced human knowledge and experience calls for a more highly creative activity. There may be occasions when even the *mode* of analyzing, grouping and defining the phenomena are at first unknown and must be discovered. This change of mode involves re-assessing what are the invariant concepts upon which to base further knowledge. Thus the separate conservation of mass and energy becomes a single conserved entity mass-energy, and similarly space and time become space-time.

When this mode is discovered its formal and structural properties must also be understood. An explanatory principle can be arrived at by specific ways, as in nuclear physics in the 'principle of asymmetry' among certain particles acted on by the 'weak' sub-nuclear forces.

Here we have a world where the mirror image does not exist and where one cannot conceive of the reversal of time (Charap, 1965). Such conceptual restrictions carry with them formal restrictions in any algebra designed to describe and amplify argument about further consequences. The complex and rapidly developing notions of conservation and invariance in the sub-nuclear world raise at a very advanced level the type of question Piaget asks about children's notions of invariance of the simpler fundamentals of reality such as substance, weight, time, etc. (Noyes, 1957). According to our notion of what is invariant during change, so we shape a concept and the formal and structural properties associated with it.

The mature learner may have all the unmediated perceptual categories established together with a full knowledge of the formal machinery of classification but still have to find adequate categories for some of the unusual collections of data found in the sciences. These will have to be sought and since the attributes are not nicely mapped out for him, the investigator may in his search come up against the problem of separating out different subclasses to obtain an adequate structure. More rarely but perhaps not so infrequently as usually assumed, he may have to look for quite novel modes of giving meaning to observations he has to interpret and may be called to elucidate the formal properties of such modes.

Here is an example to illustrate how the adolescent and adult have to deal with intellectual data for which they may have no ready-made attributes and concepts. I ask the reader to explain the data I shall now provide and to do this he will form certain concepts.

We asked 70 students to complete the following sentence by putting two words in the blank spaces:

At the end of the visit, because the children were hungry and tired we ...... make them wash their hands before eating.

Twenty of the students had English as their native language. Their replies have a small n written after each one. The other 50 had acquired English as a second language. Here are the replies:

did not (n), could not, failed to, did not, had to, need not, ought to, did not, decide to, tell and, did not (n), could not, had to (n), neglected to (n), have to, did not (n), ordered to, had to, try to, did not (n), did not, decide to, had to, could not (n), did not (n), could not, do not (n), decided to, had to, could not, could not, did not, did not (n), had to, failed to, had to (n), did not (n), had to, did not (n), did not, do not (n), could not, ought to, have to, could not, had to, did not, did not (n), did not (n), could not, had to, tried to, must do, did not (n), had to, could not, agreed to, will never, did not, teachers ourselves, did not (n), had to, did not, will not, had to (n), did not (n).

Four students did not attempt the question.

In the above problem there is no question of asking the reader to match categories supplied to him by the research worker. The reader has to find workable categories for his own solution and as he does so he is constantly reminded of the need to deal with inclusion of classes by higher ranking ones and of the need to exclude classes of equal rank from each other.

The reader's solution, based on his conceptualizing of the material, may not be the same as that of the author, whose solution appears in Appendix 7.

The task was given to a group of students and teachers most of whom tested first enumerated the frequency of different answers and then broke these down according to whether they were made by persons having English as their mother tongue or as their second language. Thereafter appeared such interpretations as the following, in terms of concepts formed by the solvers. Ability to conceptualize varied widely. Here are two extreme solutions:

Person A—analyzed the material adequately and formed concepts concerning the attitudes of the subjects of the test.

English as native language
The majority of replies (13 out of 20)=did not.
The thought of tiredness and hunger was foremost in their minds and the need for clean hands was not significant in their minds.

English as second language
1 Had to=10 out of 46 replies. The need for clean hands before eating was significant to these people despite the hunger and tiredness.
2 Could not=9 out of 46 replies. This shows thought about trying to make them wash their hands but the hunger and tiredness of the children made the attempt unsuccessful.

3 Did not=8 out of 46 replies. (As for English as native language.)

4 12 out of 46 replies=showed thought about trying to make them wash. (These are additional to the above.)

Conclusion

The English-as-second-language students showed more evidence of thought about trying to make them wash their hands than the English-as-native-language students who placed tiredness and hunger first.

Person H	—was not successful in forming explanatory concepts.
Did not	—they didn't wash their hands, people understand.
Could not	—impossible, hadn't the ability to make them.
Failed to	—failed in the attempt to make them.
Had to	—necessary to make them
Need not	—was necessary for them to wash their hands.
Ought to	—thought it necessary, but did not make them.
Decided to	—came to a decision because they were tired.
Tell and	—told them, then make them.
Neglected to	—people forgot to make them.
Ordered to	—told them in straight terms.
Try to	—tried without success.
Do not	—present tense, never make them.
Have to	—always have to make them.
Tried to	—attempted to make them unsuccessfully.
Must do	—always think it is necessary.
Agreed to	—came to a decision to make them.

In all, the replies, semantic, grammatical and logical concepts, were formed with varying degrees of success and precision.

Here is another example from experimental investigations on the nature of heat which can be tried with young secondary school pupils who have not had formal instruction in the physics of heat.

Study the following experiments and their results and then write down what they tell you about hot and cold objects.

1 Hold a piece of cold iron. Note the sensation in your hand and feel its temperature with your other hand.

2 A piece of iron was weighed cold and then heated and whilst still hot weighed again. No change in weight was found.

3 When a hot piece of iron is placed in cold water, the water gets warmer and iron gets colder until both iron and water are at the same temperature.

4 If one end of a copper rod is heated which has small dabs of paraffin wax stuck on it at intervals they melt in turn beginning at the heated end.

Most pupils arrive at the pre-Joule concept of heat as a weightless fluid.

We may close this section by a brief account of a brilliant piece of concept formation in contemporary scholarship. It was performed by Ventres when he deciphered the Cretan language found on hundreds of tablets discovered by archaeologists and called Linear B (Chadwick, 1958). It was outstanding because here was an unknown language in an unknown script. Here is a drawing of one of the clay tablets into which the script had been cut by a stylus.

Figure 8

A Knossos chariot tablet (sc 230)

Novel as this task seems to the layman it illustrates a modification we must make to the view that when expert thinkers are confronted with such a problem they are wholly concerned with concept formation and not at all with concept attainment. In such cases as in the instance taken from vocabulary used by native and non-native English speakers, the thinker really both forms and attains concepts. He does the latter if he has any significant background to work from. Thus in the case of the decipherment of Linear B, the first task was to determine the nature of the script. Was it ideographic like Chinese or ancient Egyptian, where one sign stands for one idea? Was it syllabic, where each sign stands for a syllable? Or was it alphabetic, where each sign stands for a letter? These are concepts to be attained since they are already formulated and it is not difficult for a professional to settle this point. All he needs to do is to count the number of different signs. Linear B was found to be syllabic. It contained also some ideographs but these were relatively easy to pick out.

From this point the slow process of formation of concepts proceeded until finally a concept was attained which the workers knew about but had not thought feasible—that the language was an archaic form of Greek!

Other concepts had to be formed and there is still much to be explained, but the major interpretation seems beyond doubt.

vi THREE PARTS OF A CONCEPT

When viewed as a psychologically finished product, a concept has three aspects all of which play important roles in the growth of thinking. Ideas like working class or mediterranean climate imply first some general property, as to what conditions any individual instance of the working class, etc., have to fulfil for membership. Such a definition forms the *intensive* aspect of the concept. The *extensive* aspect, forming a second feature, is seen in the actual set of individuals forming the basis of the concept. In much secondary school and college learning in the humanities a single instance only may be discussed in context. This use of contextual clues about a single instance can produce difficulties as will be shown. Thirdly, the concept has its name which symbolises or identifies the concept. Names may be wholly arbitrary, as in -x in the set of negative whole numbers, or more relevant, as in *working class*—but in essence they are identifying tags.

Experimental psychologists have used all three components variously in investigating the formation of concepts. When an experimenter uses the Vygotsky blocks he is providing the child with the names BIK, CEV, etc., and with the extensive array of material. The child has to provide the rule or defining properties symbolized by the particular name. In typical concept learning experiments using coloured shapes on cards with immediate feedback as to whether the particular card exposed is an instance of the concept to be discovered or not, the extensive array of instances, together with the array of non-instances is given and the learner has to recognize instances and then often has to formulate the intensive rule which makes them so. Educational research on the child's concepts in school subjects such as history or geography often start simply from the name: What is a king? Werner and Kaplan (op. cit.) used six instances each of arbitrarily named concepts and the thinker had to produce a definition.

In education the name or symbol for a concept may cause difficulties, particularly if the learners are not reminded frequently enough what is symbolized. Algebra is prone to symbol domination. Much of its elementary study is concerned with the manipulation of concepts in a deductive way by using the symbol as the manipuland. If the symbol and the abstract structure which it symbolizes become too detached mistakes often arise. This is probably the commonest cause of errors in algebra among mid-adolescents.

Some of the difficulties met in forming historical concepts when the learner has only an unfamiliar name embedded in a textual setting were well brought out by De Silva (1969) who chose ten concept terms used in history, including the words *monopoly*, *slump* (*or depression*), *tariff*, *capital*, *nationalism*, and then selected contexts from school history texts each of which contained between 80–100 words and in which the concept word occurred once. It was then coded by a 'word' unknown to the subjects, e.g., SLUMP = MALMIR. The subjects were asked: What is X...? Why do you think so? Here is one of the passages:

RAMUDAL (capital)

The new trading enterprises in Tudor and Stuart times were different from the overseas enterprises of mediaeval times. The countries traded with were farther away than Flanders and France. The journeys to be made were, therefore, much more dangerous; the time occupied over a single journey was very much longer than had been formerly the case. Hence *ramudal* became a very important factor in these enterprises and almost the whole trade ultimately passed under the control of vast concerns.

Using a scheme of analysis of the answers based on previous work on the understanding of short textual passages*, De Silva grouped

---

* See Chapter 2.

his answers according to categories as follows: logically restricted, circumstantial conceptualization, logical possibilities, deductive conceptualization.

Logically restricted answers are tautological, inconsistent, directly contradictory, irrelevant or otherwise irrational and display a gross lack of comprehension of the passage.

Examples were:
The word 'ramudal' means that something is a very important thing.
(Age 13)
A government or high official;
Because it became so important. (Age 13)

Circumstantial conceptualization is an attempt at understanding based on a single piece of circumstantial evidence picked out from the context supporting a simple unqualified inference. Subjects do not show signs of being able to use all the material clues given and are content with very limited, trivial responses.

Examples were:
Canals;
The canals help to get to a place by a shorter route like the Egyptian one. (Age 14)
Water or food;
Because earlier in the passage it said trips were taking longer. (Age 14)

Logical possibilities—realistic appraisal showing capacity to combine two or more pieces of evidence and ability to relate cause and effect. Possible alternatives and competing solutions are offered and possible explanations invoked. However, they do not stand against all the facts of the situation.

Examples were:
I think 'ramudal' means exploration;
I think this because if the journeys were long and dangerous then a new route, shorter and involving less complications would have to be found. (Age 13)

Ramudal probably means trading companies;
This is probably so because at this time trading was becoming

too difficult to be handled by individuals so companies like the East India Company were set up. (Age 15)

Deductive conceptualization explores the content of the passage in almost its entirety in a deductive way and draws integrated, reasoned, penetrating and imagined inference taking account essentially of the problem ... deductive reasoning or sustained argument from the basis of assumed hypotheses.

Examples were:
Money;
I think so because the long journeys made during trading would cost much more than they did before. Also the phrase 'passed under the control of vast concerns' makes me think that money is the word. (Age 16)
Capital;
A vast concern usually produces 'capital'. The reference to the time of the journeys and the dangers involved lead me to come upon 'capital'. For capital would be needed to withstand the time taken in the journeys, also to buy the large numbers of goods, also to replace the goods or ships lost in the journey. (Age 16)

De Silva tested 80 grammar and 80 non-grammar type pupils in a comprehensive school across the age range of 12 to 16 years. The percentage frequencies of responses in the different answer categories were as follows:

Table XXVI Percentages of Frequency

Answer category	Age	12	13	14	15	16
	no.	20	40	40	40	20
No response		4·0	3·5	6·5	9·5	5·5
Logically restricted		71·0	68·8	63·0	47·0	40·0
Circumstantial Conceptualization		10·0	9·3	10·5	15·5	16·5
Logical possibility		4·5	6·0	4·3	8·8	3·5
Deductive Conceptualization		10·5	12·5	15·8	19·0	34·5

We may note the diminishing but continued high frequence of logically restricted answers and the rising frequency of deductive responses. Only at 16 does there appear to be a significant appearance of concept formation at the most mature level.

vii GENERALIZATION AND ABSTRACTION

Earlier in this chapter (p. 130) we noted the importance of abstractions in any discourse in which explanations and judgments were being made.

We now consider the adolescents' power to make abstractions, but before describing the results of testing this power I shall need to examine the circumstances in which the act of generalizing and abstracting differ (Peel, 1971).

These terms are frequently used in an interchangeable sense as when people talk of abstracting a rule or generalizing into a law. But on the whole psychologists think of generalization as applying to the extensive array of instances embodying the concept and use such terms as extending the generalization to include fresh instances. The word is used in this sense in the present text.

The word abstraction takes over some ambiguity from the two grammatical meanings of the word *abstract*. First, as an adjective in such expressions as 'this is too abstract' it may mean that the range of instances is too diverse for a concrete picture to be easy. A theory may also be considered very abstract if it is difficult to imagine a suggestive instance. When used as an adjective *abstract* is really equivalent to *general*.

But when we say we *abstract* a rule, definition or law we use the word in the intensive sense of finding the essential properties which define the concept. The equivalent meaning of *abstraction* is accepted for use here.

There is a lot to be gained by distinguishing between generalization and abstraction in this way as being equivalent respectively to the extensive and intensive features of a concept. A generalization really becomes a concept only when it is capable of being abstracted in a communicable rule.

Confusion often arises because there are many instances in the English language where the same word denotes both a generalization

K

and an abstraction. Take for example the word *church* and consider the following sentences:

a St. Michael's, Boldmere, is a church,
b a church is a place of worship,
c church is a religious idea,
d the church forbids it.

Here we have church used in four ways: as a particular building, a place of worship, an idea, and as an institution. No wonder some history teachers avoid using the word.

We can use the above example to make clear distinction between generalizing and abstracting. First we separate out increasing degrees of generalization beginning with the particular, from levels of abstraction beginning with the concrete.

For any object or class* let us postulate g_0, g_1, g_2 . . . degrees of generalisation, where g_0 is the particular case, i.e., of zero generalization, and the suffixes 1, 2 . . . indicate increasing degrees.

For the same object or class let us postulate a_0, a_i, a_{ii} levels of abstraction where a_0 is the concrete case, i.e., of zero abstraction, and the suffixes i, ii . . . indicate rising levels of abstraction. Then any term forming the subject or its predicate in a logical sentence can be described in two ways, according to how abstract and generalized it is. Thus in the sentence: *Attila was an aggressor*, Attila is symbolized by a_0, g_0 and aggressor by a_0, g_1. In a logical sentence the subject and its predicate are always at the same level of abstraction but the predicate is more general.

Let us consider sentences a and b above
St. Michael's, Boldmere is concrete and particular (a_0, g_0),
church is concrete but general (a_0, g_1),
place of worship is still concrete but is even more general (a_0, g_2).

Here we have increasing degrees of generalization but no change from the concrete. The reader may also notice that the inclusions embodied in these two sentences are transitive, that is: St. Michael's is a place of worship.

Now let us examine sentences a and c. We notice now that in c the meaning of church has changed. It is no longer a concrete general

* We may also include attributes and relationships but for the moment I limit the development of the argument to the case of objects and classes.

term including St. Michael's, St. Peter's, All Saints, etc., but is symbolizing the idea of church. It is now abstract and particular (a_1, g_0) and its predicate, *religious idea,* is at the same level of abstraction but is more general. It is therefore symbolized by (a_1, g_1).

We may also note that the relationships expressed in a and c are not transitive, that is, the material building, St. Michael's, Boldmere, is not a religious idea.

I can now say what I mean by the act of abstracting and the consequent result, an abstraction. When a person shifts an idea from its concrete general form (a_0, g_1) to its abstract particular equivalent (a_1, g_0) then he engages in the process of abstraction.

A word like *church* which symbolizes both meanings is a homonym in a special covert sense since it is the common name for two forms of the same idea. We can utilize this fact in order to test the prevalence during adolescence of abstraction, as defined above, in comparison with that of generalization.

This can be done by leading the thinker from the concrete-particular to the concrete-general and then to call for a response at a third level. This third level is tested by a multiple-choice form, incorporating possible responses which individually involve generalization, abstraction, constituent parts and partial associations. Here is a prototype instance. The subject is asked to underline the word or phrase in the column on the right which he thinks most appropriately completes the row of three terms.

Kilimanjaro (a_0, g_0) volcanic peak (a_0, g_1) mountain (a_0, g_2)
                                     (a_1, g_0) Tanzania (partial
                                                              association)
                                                          geological notion
                                                              (a_1, g_1)
                                                          snowcap (irrelevant
                                                              constituent part)
                                                          highest mountain in
                                                              Africa (partial
                                                              association)

If the subject underlines mountain he is generalizing further from volcanic peak. Hence I infer that the meaning of volcanic peak is taken to be in the concrete-general form (a_0, g_1). If he underlines geological notion then I assume he is using volcanic peak in its abstract sense (a_i, g_o). The choice of Tanzania, snowcap or highest mountain in Africa would indicate restricted logical activity.

A test of twenty items similar to the above prototype was given to groups of 12-year-old and 16-year-old secondary school pupils of not more than average ability and a group of adult students of superior mental ability.

In the analysis of their replies we are able to group the responses into three categories: A-responses (abstractions), G-responses (generalizations) and O-responses (others). The frequencies in these response categories and the equivalent percentages are given in Table XXVII.

Table XXVII Frequency and percentages of A, G and O responses

Group	n	A	G	O	Total responses
Adult	32	248	278	114	640
%		38·8	43·4	17·8	
16 year olds	30	87	271	242	600
%		14·5	45·2	40·3	
12 year olds	33	58	283	319	660
%		8·8	42·9	48·3	

The youngest group makes only 8·8 per cent A-responses, and there is a steady rise in the percentage of A-responses as we consider older groups. There is a large difference between the 16-year-olds and the 21+-year-old postgraduate group. There is more than an age difference to bear in mind. The 16-year-old group was if anything of slightly less than average ability while the adult group was composed of people highly selected on intellectual ability. We need to look at 16-, 17- and 18-year-old groups of perhaps greater ability, but the trend is clear that the power to abstract appears more evident in the older groups. Also unlogical responses (O-responses) are less frequent in older people. On the surface the overall tendency to make G-responses seems to be constant, but this may not be a static situation. It could be due to a shift from O to G to A responses.

We may test the significance of the trend towards more abstract responses with age by calculating the mean A scores for each of the three age groups and comparing them by using the Standard Error of the difference between two means.

The A score means and standard deviations are given in Table XXVIII:

Table XXVIII A Scores

Group	12 yr	16 yr	Adult
Mean	1·76	2·90	7·72
Standard Deviation	1·50	1·60	3·13
Critical Ratios of SE differences of means to actual differences		16 – 12 yr 2·91	Adult – 16 yr 7·71

We may assume therefore a real difference between the capacity of each of the three groups to form abstractions.

viii SUMMING UP

In this chapter I have tried to show that adolescent concept formation presents problems peculiar to adolescence. These centre around the circumstances in which concepts are formed, as for example in verbal contexts, and the complexity of the concepts themselves.

In some instances we need more information about how adolescent and adult thinkers build up concepts. This applies to relational concepts when the relationships have to be discovered by the thinker.

In forming entirely new concepts three capacities may be called for: deciding upon the attributes and their values, a knowledge of the formal properties of the acts carried out to form the attributes, and, more rarely, a readiness to reconsider what entities may be conserved or remain invariant and a power to deduce the consequences of such changes in conservation. Much might be done to investigate the adolescent's creative powers in novel situations.

However, in spite of these gaps we have provided evidence to show that the adolescent may be limited in forming superordinate classes when using verbal material restricted to the names and descriptions of classes.

We have also discussed the psychological significance of the extensive array, the intensive definition and the name of a concept and have shown how difficult it is to find a concept if given only its name embedded in an extensional context made up largely of one instance.

Finally, we have attempted to differentiate between the acts of generalizing and abstracting and have suggested and tried an empirical method of testing the capacity of the adolescent to carry out these acts. We have found he generalizes more readily than he abstracts but that abstracting is a noticeably growing feature of the thinking of the late adolescent and adult.

CHAPTER EIGHT

The Adolescent Intellect

The aims of this monograph were introduced by a statement of a belief about the basic characteristic of adolescent thought—the capacity to invoke the possible and the attendant mental act of setting it against the actual. This leads the young person to explain and judge and also, in so far as he can, to take action to attempt to modify the actualities of his existence. The purpose of the research described and the views advanced and tested has been to show how the first two powers, of explaining and judging develop as the individual grows into adulthood. I attempt now to sum up these findings about the mental growth of the adolescent.

First we have the general picture suggested by the foregoing series of research studies. We can expect the capacity to imagine possibilities in the minority only before the ages 13–15. Over this range of mind-adolescence there is a rapid acceleration in the power to offer explanations and make judgments, so that thereafter we have a majority capacity. But as far into adulthood as we have tested there always appears a residue of thinkers incapable of offering adequate explanations or making mature judgments.

The intellectual evaluations of younger adolescents are dominated by circumstantial and descriptive comment limited to the here and now. Several factors are related to the onset of the period of change, from what I have called circumstantial descriptive thought to imaginative explanation.

First, there are the qualities of the young thinker, his age, mental ability, socio-economic level, and maturity of language usage, including the capacity to use language to express abstract thought. All these characteristics are positively associated with the growth of mature explanation and judgment.

Instruction in how to think and judge appears to improve the quality of judgment but an element of readiness may also be a condition for such improvement. Research on the effect of adding information to problem passages shows that once a person is capable of imagining and invoking possibilities he will tend to do so in all circumstances. It appears to be more than a matter of mere availability of information. The information must be structured in the thinker's intellect and he must have the attitude to knowledge that assumes the value of his own contribution.

Problems of a social and culturally familiar kind are more readily judged in a mature way than are non-social and more technical problems. Where problem material has been so designed as to test the power to follow strict logical argument, it has been found that the very ablest thinkers react rigorously to logical and linguistic form but also that many able people will make assumptions about omissions and then offer imaginative explanations. This adventuresome quality of thought is important and links with the general feature of adolescent intelligence mentioned earlier.

Lastly, the form of question can influence the judgment. When we challenge the adolescent with a problem situation by asking what problem he sees, rather than by directing his attention to an aspect of the situation, he answers on the same scale of judgment from partial circumstantial replies to imaginative comprehensive judgments but at a slightly lower level.

Investigations of the relationship between personality variables, extraversion–introversion and stability–neuroticism and maturity of judgment have so far not revealed any consistent feaures. However these enquiries have been rather tentative and more thorough experiments might well be tried out.

So far, the act of judgment, measured by responses to problem situations, has been compared with other variables stemming from the thinker's personal qualities and background, the effect of instruction, the nature of the problem passages and the form of evoking a judgment.

We can also break down the act of judgment into its components and compare the maturity of the judger in these specific aspects with the dominant correlates of chronological and mental age. The act of judgment has been broken down into the following parts:

Arousal of the process,
Imagining and formulating hypotheses,
Selecting the most appropriate and rejecting others,
Hypothetico-deductive reasoning.

Arousal of the process of judgment is linked with intellectual curiosity which at its highest level reveals itself in the possible explanations and hypotheses posed to account for the incongruencies and dissonancies experienced by the thinker in a problem situation.

As to the imagination and formulation of hypotheses we found good quality thinking, where all elements of the situation are explored in relation to a hypothesis, only at ages of 14+. The number of hypotheses offered to explain problems correlated markedly with age and general mental ability and up to 13–14 years of age the average thinker will not produce more than one or two hypotheses. This limit links also with the apparent incapacity of the younger adolescent thinker to deal with more than one piece of evidence at a time.

The complete act of thought of selecting and rejecting hypotheses provides a severe test of thinking for all but the most able and mature adolescent thinkers. The main difficulty is the incapacity of the less mature thinkers to hold more than one hypothesis in mind and to discuss a problem situation comprehensively in terms of all possibilities. The capacity for comprehensive selection and rejection of possibilities seems to emerge only in late adolescence and early adulthood.

The ability to reason deductively from hypotheses offered to explain problem material shows itself in the power to maintain a sustained argument. It does not appear to be marked until ages of 15 and upwards.

High-level explanations entail the invocation of concepts. Adolescents usually have to form new concepts through the medium of language and one-instance descriptions. Verbal tests show that in adolescents of average ability there is still a marked proportion up to the age of 15 having difficulty in forming and recognizing logical classes, the bases of concepts. Where new concepts are introduced in textual material we find partially and circumstantially dominated inferences up to the ages of 14 and 15. By devising test material which enables one to distinguish between concrete-general and abstract-particular responses it has been possible also to show that the tendency to abstract is revealed only in a small minority in mid-adolescence. The preference is generally for generalizing or even forming partial, contiguous but illogical connections.

Finally, some hints have been obtained about the adolescent's sensitivity to the elements of change and dynamic equilibrium implied in practically every problem involving individuals and their environment and the interplay of physical, chemical and biological forces. Using archaeological, geographical and ecological material it has been shown that such sensitivity is a characteristic of more mature adolescent thinking. This tendency however needs more extensive investigation.

Because these changes in the quality of intellect during mid-adolescence are revealed wholly in the verbal medium they may appear to some to be less dramatic than the changes in earlier childhood thinking. But they are none the less extremely potent, for they lay the foundations for the penetrative and creative thought and action which may characterize adult activity.

Before this sharp gradient of intellectual growth we have, with younger adolescents, a thinker still largely dependent upon and restricted to the here and now. After it we have one who deliberates outwards and forwards and is capable of reaching to the limits of knowledge. We may well call this burgeoning the golden age of intellectual growth.

Appendices

A Sample of Judgment Test Items

ABSTRACTED FROM BRYDON (OP. CIT.)

At the present day many people die from cancer. Cigarette smoking is said to be the cause of lung cancer and yet tobacco is freely sold throughout the country. Any person over the age of 16 years can spend as much money as he likes on buying cigarettes.

Should cigarette smoking be banned by the government?

Modern youth does not show any respect for authority today. Until recently boys of 18 years of age had to serve their country doing what was known as National Service. This meant that they had to be prepared to defend the country. A man is not recognized as being an adult until he is 21 years of age, when he is allowed to vote. If there was another war, all boys of 18 years would have to go and fight.

Should young people under 21 years be allowed to take part in running the affairs of this country by being allowed to vote?

Only courageous captains are allowed to sail boats in bad weather. This summer a man who had been the captain of a warship was sailing a small boat carrying too many passengers. The boat rammed a partly submerged wreck and sank immediately. Many of the passengers died and some spent all night in the sea before being rescued.

Was the captain to blame?

Most young people want to be able to drive a car. There are too many cars on the roads already in this country and more drivers would only make the position worse.

Should young people be given lessons on driving in their last year at school?

ABSTRACTED FROM ANDERSON (OP. CIT.)

Each year the number of accidents rises and hundreds of people are killed or seriously injured on the roads. Many of the new buildings in London are very high and last week a man fell from the tenth floor of a tall block and died on the pavement below.

Is it dangerous to live in tall buildings? Why do you say that?

When Jill started work she saved some of her money in order to take her young sister, Ann, for a holiday in Scotland. During this holiday the girls went for a walk in the hills and Ann carried the haversack containing their lunch and their coats. The path was slippery and Ann stumbled, dropping the haversack down a steep cliff. They looked down at it and Jill said, 'I've a good mind to throw you down to get it.'

Was Jill kind to her sister? How do you know?

It takes a lot of strength and determination to be a champion runner; many people train and try hard but few succeed. Carol was a tall, strong girl who had always wanted to represent her school at the County Sports. She trained hard and won her race in the preliminary heats. But on the morning of the sports she slipped and sprained her ankle so that she could not take part in the finals.

Would Carol have won the finals? How do you know?

Two men were arguing about a new road to be built in their town. One said, 'It is a terrible thing! Why should we spend thousands of pounds and spoil the countryside just so that a few selfish motorists can dash along at sixty miles an hour! And think how many people are likely to be killed on the roads this year.' The other man said, 'I am glad they are building this road, I will be able to take my family to the seaside much more quickly.'

Should new roads be built? Why do you say that?

ABSTRACTED FROM MILLETT (OP. CIT.)

An aeroplane crash-lands on a coral island and the survivors, a party of schoolboys, find themselves castaways in ideal surroundings. At first they treat the situation with enthusiasm and all goes well. But later they begin to argue amongst themselves and eventually act like little savages towards one another. (William Golding, *The Lord of the Flies*.)

Why do you think the schoolboys began to argue amongst themselves? What is your opinion about these boys?

It was high summer and the boy was lying in the corn. He was happy because he had no work to do and the weather was hot. He heard the corn sway from side to side above him and the noise of the birds who whistled from the branches of the trees that hid the house. Lying flat on his back he stared up into the unbrokenly blue sky falling over the edge of the corn. (Dylan Thomas, *A Prospect of the Sea*.)

Was the boy lazy? What do you think about the boy?

He was an old man who fished alone in a skiff in the Gulf Stream and he had gone eighty-four days now without taking a fish. In the first forty days a boy had been with him. But after forty days without a fish the boy's parents had told him that the old man was now definitely and finally 'solao', which is the worst form of unlucky and the boy had gone at their orders in another boat which caught three good fish the first week. (Ernest Hemingway, *The Old Man and the Sea*.)

Was the old man a good fisherman? What do you think about this old fisherman?

A Selected Test Item from Rhys (op. cit.)

The passage was taken from a school text and is perhaps longer than necessary for the purpose of the test, but it conveys a good geographical problem setting.

Antonio Arango invested his life-savings in the purchase of a fifty-acre plot of land in the Magdalena Valley, high up amongst the slopes of the Andes in South America. The land was covered with tall timber, which showed the fertility of the soil. 'Where such big trees grow, the soil is good,' said Antonio to himself, and he gazed with satisfaction at the thick layer of vegetable top-soil which could be seen in the cutting made by the brook. The water of the brook was crystal clear, so crystalline that Antonio and his sons christened it Diamond Brook.

Antonio sharpened his axe, the iron that was to conquer the woodland. The timber, when it had been cut, could not be used because there were no roads by which to remove it nor neighbouring towns to buy it. So he let a few days' sunshine dry the fallen leaves and then set fire to them. Other settlers were doing the same in other parts of the mountains. The blaze was enormous.

At long last the ground was cleared and Antonio sowed it with maize, keeping five acres as pasture for his cow. And, on the high ground he built a house, too. Antonio named the house after his wife, *La Isabella*. The first harvest was encouraging. Antonio was well pleased with his efforts, so he went on sowing maize. But things were changing.

Diamond Brook, which had once been brimming and crystal-clear throughout the year, had shrunk to a thread of water in summer-time. In the rainy season it was a yellow flood tearing loose rocks and mud and lumps of soil. The harvests were growing smaller. Antonio sold the cow because the pasture was no longer enough for it to live on. Things were not going right for him at all. One day, when he was sowing maize, his spade struck solid rock. The vegetable topsoil had become so thin that already rocky out-crops were appearing everywhere. There was no money in the house. The children had nothing to eat. Lastly, Diamond Brook vanished and only its stony channel was left. Like so many other settlers, Antonio Arango sought another stretch of woodland to begin again.

Rhys asked three questions of which the following was the first:

Question 1: Why did the deep fertile soil cover disappear and make farming impossible?

Grading by Different Assessors

Categories

| | | *Restricted* | *Circumstantial* | *Imaginative* |

*R   No. The train spotters will have nothing to do.

```
       X
       X
      X X
1 *G  X X X X    X    X        X
      A                   B                    C
```

R   Yes. Then Lynn will not be so busy.

```
          X      X   X
2 G   X X X X    X   X   X X
                         |
```

R   No. Because the people cannot do their shopping.

```
                          X
                     X   X X
       X        X    X   X X X      X
3 G    X             X              |
```

R   No. The people of Burton may depend on Lynn for their shopping.

```
                               X
                               X
                              X X          X
4 G                  X X      X X X         X
                              |
```

R   Yes. People should do their shopping in their own town and this is good for trade.

```
                          X
                          X
5 G   X   X       X    X X X    X   X
                               X
                               |
```

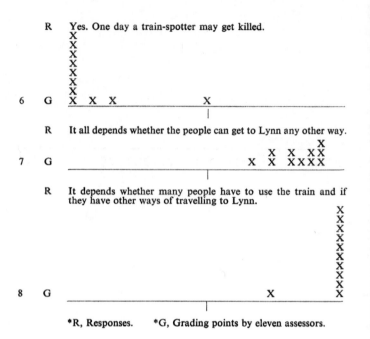

R   Yes. One day a train-spotter may get killed.

6   G

R   It all depends whether the people can get to Lynn any other way.

7   G

R   It depends whether many people have to use the train and if they have other ways of travelling to Lynn.

8   G

*R, Responses.   *G, Grading points by eleven assessors.

A Selection of Test Material from Anderson (op. cit.) Showing the Open and Multiple-choice Form of asking a Question on each Problem Passage

Eight such passages were used in all.

Passage 2
It takes a lot of strength and determination to be a champion runner. Many people train and try hard but few succeed. Carol was a tall, strong girl who had always wanted to represent her school at the County Sports. She trained hard and won her race in the preliminary heats. But on the morning of the sports she slipped and sprained her ankle so that she could not take part in the finals.

Questions: A. Would Carol have won the final?
B. How do you know?

Multiple-choice alternatives:
(Question, would Carol have won the final?)

1 Carol would have won the finals because of all the hard training she had done.

2 Carol would have won the race because it was only an accident that she slipped and she was a tall, strong girl and very determined to win.

3 You cannot tell because she didn't run in the final.

4   Carol may have won the final because she had already won
     several other races.

5   Carol would not win because she would be nervous.

Passage 4

Jane is a very clever fifteen-year-old girl who is preparing for her
final examinations. One evening, as Jane was doing her homework,
her mother asked her to look after her younger brother, David,
while she went out. David wandered from the living-room into
the kitchen, got hold of a jar of jam, ate a lot of it, covered his
clothes with it, and spilled it on to some clean washing in a basket
so that it was ruined.

Questions: A. Was Jane a careless person?

                B. Why do you think so?

Multiple-choice alternatives:
(Question, was Jane a careless person?)

1   Jane was careless not to watch David as well as doing her
     homework.

2   Jane was not careless because her mother should not have
     expected her to watch David as well as doing her important
     homework.

3   If Jane hadn't been careless she would not have allowed David
     to wander into the kitchen.

4   Jane was a very careless girl to let her brother make those clean
     clothes all dirty and sticky.

5   Jane is not careless because she is clever.

Passage 5

Miss James is a strict teacher whose classes work well because she
insists on school rules being obeyed. For some time now she has
been learning to drive and has had some trouble in changing gears.
She will be taking her driving-test next month.

Questions: A. Will Miss James pass her driving test?

                B. How do you know?

Multiple-choice alternatives:
(Question, will Miss James pass her driving test?)

1   You cannot tell until she takes it.

2   She will not pass because she may change gear badly and cause an accident.

3   She will pass because she is strict and keeps to the rules.

4   She will not pass because she won't be thinking what she is doing, but only about being strict at school.

5   She may pass because she is a good teacher and so she will obey the Highway Code.

Excerpts from the Programmed Thinking Sequence Based on The 'Pilot' Problem (Gray, op. cit.)

Read the following passage:

page 1

Only brave pilots are allowed to fly over high mountains. One summer a fighter pilot, flying over the Alps, collided with an aerial cable-way, and cut a main cable, causing some cars to fall to the glacier below. Several people were killed and many others had to spend the night suspended above the glacier.

page 2

Question: Was the pilot a careful airman?

Select your answer from the following:
1 Yes, the cable should not have been there.
Turn to page 3

2 No, because he hit the cable.
Turn to page 14

3 Yes, he may have flown into a bank of mist that obscured his vision.
Turn to page 21

page 3

Your answer: Yes, the cable should not have been there.
It was very unfortunate that the aerial cable-way stretched directly

across the pilot's course. BUT such a hazard to aeroplanes would certainly be marked on the maps used by pilots.

When a pilot plans his route, he notes very carefully the height and exact location of ALL obstructions which could possibly endanger his safety.

Is it really fair to judge the pilot on the basis of the presence of an aerial cable-way?

Here again is the question:

Was the pilot a careful airman?

Select your answer from the following:

1   Yes, because he was brave.   Turn to page   4.

2   No, because he must have been showing off.   Turn to page   7.

3   No, because if he had been careful, he would
    have avoided the cable.   Turn to page 11.

page 14

Your Answer: NO, because he hit the cable.

Certainly he hit the cable.

Was it deliberate? A suicide? A criminal act, say, to kill someone in an aerial car? (a jilted lover?) We don't know but there are perhaps more likely possibilities.

What we are trying to decide at this moment is, 'Was the pilot a careless airman?'

Make your selection from the following:

1   If the pilot had been careful he would have
    made a safe flight over the mountain.   Turn to page 15

2   Because the aircraft crashed, we can say that
    the pilot was careless.   Turn to page 16.

3   No, because a freak downdraught of air may
    have momentarily taken control of the aircraft.

                                                   Turn to page 17.

page 21

Your Answer: YES, He may have flown into a bank of mist
               that obscured his vision.

M

You are right to consider the possibility that the pilot flew into mist.

Would this necessarily indicate carelessness on the part of the pilot?

1 Yes   Turn to page 22.

2 No   Turn to page 23.

Excerpts from an Inquiry into Secondary School Pupils' Historical Judgments (Stones, op. cit.)

During the last century most of the western civilised countries increased their population and wealth but no country grew more rapidly in this respect than America. During the years between 1830 and 1900 the population of the United States grew to over 76 million. Many of the people came from the British Isles and Europe to settle and make a new life in this vast, exciting country. During this period an enormous network of railways was built up covering the entire country until the railway system of America was greater than that covering the whole of Europe. Oil wells, coal mines, and steel making factories grew up so quickly that they almost seemed to spring up overnight. Gradually America became a nation capable of producing a great range of manufactured goods, great quantities of food and a never ending stream of ideas and inventions. The America of the farmer, the cowboy and the frontier town changed to the America we know today and with it changed the lives of all those varied people who populated this enormous country.

What exactly was this change and how did it come about? Probably the most important fact to consider was the improvement in transport brought about by the building of the railway network. Before the railways were built there was vast areas of America which had no roads, canals or rivers. They were constructed with the most astonishing speed and energy and succeeded in linking up

171

the distant parts of the country. They gradually helped to spread similar tastes and habits of people who came from many different backgrounds and countries. But most important of all, especially to the many factory towns, the railways created one enormous market for both fool and mass produced goods. Through the railways a factory owner could hope to sell his goods all over America, whereas previously he would have been restricted to his own town and surrounding district. The farmers who had been able to settle out East and start their farms because of the railway links, used the railways to transport their cattle, grain and food to a greater number of customers. And where the railways reached the ports like New York both farmers and factory owners were able to sell their products to other countries.

Questions:

1 Explain the connections you can see between the increase in railways in America and the inventions of methods of mass production in factories.

2 Imagine that no railways had been built during this period. What differences do you think it would have made?

3 How do you think railways could help to spread similar tastes to people from different countries?

Formation of Language Concepts

Task: Complete the following sentence by inserting two words in
the place provided:
At the end of the visit, because the children were hungry and
tired we ... ... make them wash their hands before eating.

Analysis of the answers

Response	Native English (20)	Second English (50)	Category of answer	Proportion in the Categories Nat. Eng.	Sec. Eng.
did not	13	8			
could not	1	9	1	·75	·38
failed to		2			
neglected to	1				
had to	3	10			
decided to		3	2	·15	·30
agreed to		1			
tried to		1			

do not	2				
will not		1	1a	·10	·06
need not		1			
will never		1			
have to		2			
ought to		2	2a		·12
try to		1			
teachers ourselves		1			
ordered to		1			
must to		1	2b		·06
tell and		1			
not attempted		4			·08
Total	20	50		1·00	1·00

The first thing we note is that there are two broad classes of reply, designated the 1 and 2 series, which show that the subjects started off from two opposing attitudes about hunger and cleanliness. Those people in Category 1 put hunger before cleanliness, while those people in Category 2 put cleaniless before hunger. This is a psychological or semantic element but once having cleared this away we can then look at the answers structurally. Category 1 answers are the ones we are most certain about since these replies follow structurally upon the connective *because*.

We cannot be so certain about Category 2 answers because these answers could follow upon the connective because or although.

Did this happen either

a because the subjects could not differentiate between the significance of *because* and *although* or

b because they were in fact not interested in satisfying the children's hunger until they had washed their hands? This latter attitude would make Category 2 answers quite legitimate sequences to *because*. (If, however, they were distressed by the hunger of the children and in spite of that wished to have them wash their hands, then their replies should have followed *although*.)

There is a further ambiguity in Category 2 answers which could be resolved only by taking spoken replies and looking for the stress. For instance we might have

c ... *because* the children ... we *had* to make them ...

and

d ... because the children ... we had to *make* them ....

In the case of c responses the speakers feel morally obliged but are sympathetic and moved by the children's hunger. In the case of d answers the emphasis is on the need to force the children to wash their hands.

Within both categories the replies have been graded downwards from the most neutral to the more emotionally loaded responses.

The non-grammatical sub-sections of the major categories brought out structural errors relating to tense (1a and 2a) and more involved grammatical defects in 2b.

Turning to a comparison between the two groups let us give the Category 2 answers the benefit of the doubt syntactically but thereby label them as toughminded with regard to cleanliness; that is, assume explanation b above. This may be a dubious assumption in view of the proportions of answers in Category 1, namely ·75 for the native English speakers and ·38 only for the overseas group.

It is noteworthy that the proportion of definite structural aberrations and omissions in the overseas group was more than three times that of the native speaking group (·32 as against ·10).

Bibliography

ABERCROMBIE, M. J. I., *The Anatomy of Judgment*, Hutchinson, London, 1960.

ANDERSON, D. R., An Investigation Into the Effects of Instruction on the Development of Propositional Thinking in Children. Dip. Child Psy. research, School of Education, Birmingham University, 1967.

ASHTON, P. M. E., A Study of the Curiosity of 10 and 11 Year Old Children. Unpub. Ph.D. thesis, Dept. of Education, Birmingham University, 1965.

AUSUBEL, D., *The Psychology of Meaningful Learning*, Grune and Stratton, New York, 1963.

BARTHOLOMEW, M. L., Language and judgment levels amongst first and fourth year pupils at a County Secondary School, D.C.P. Dissertation, University of Birmingham, 1970.

BEBERMAN, M., An Emerging Program of Secondary School Mathematics, *New Curricula*, p. 11, (ed. R. W. HEATH), Harper & Row, New York, 1964.

BERLYNE, D. E., *Conflict, Arousal and Curiosity*, McGraw-Hill, New York, 1960.

BEST, O. G., The Development of Explanatory Thought in the Adolescent in Out-of-School Situations. Dip. Child Psy. research, School of Education, Birmingham University, 1967.

BIRAN, L. A., Do Plants Lose Water? Unpublished programmed learning text, Birmingham University, 1968.

BLOOM, B. S., *Taxonomy of Educational Objectives,* Longmans, New York, 1956.

BOWER, E. M. and HOLLISTER, L. E., *Behavioral Science Frontiers in Education,* Wiley, New York, 1967.

BRUNER, J. S., *The Process of Education Towards a Theory of Instruction,* Harvard University Press, Cambridge, Mass., 1960.

BRUNER, J. S., OLVER, R. R. and GREENFIELD, P. M., *Studies in Cognitive Growth,* Wiley, New York, 1966.

BRYDON, J., An Investigation of Certain Factors Entering into the Judgments of Adolescent Boys and Girls. Dip. Child Psy. reserach, School of Education, Birmingham University, 1967.

CHADWICK, J., *The Decipherment of Linear B,* Cambridge University Press, 1958.

CHARAP, J. M., Towards the Quark, *Discovery,* pp. 16–21, June 1965.

CLOWES, R., *The Structure of Life,* pp. 28–38 and Chap. 10, Penguin Books, Harmondsworth, 1967.

CONNOLLY, CYRIL, Scholarship in a Soapbubble (Book review), *Sunday Times,* London, 19 April 1964.

COVINGTON, M. V. and CRUTCHFIELD, R. S., Facilitation of Creative Problem Solving: Experiments Using Programmed Instruction, 1965.

CRONBACH, L. J. and AZUMA, H., Performance on a Concept Attainment Task with Scaled Cues, University of Illinois, 1961.

CRUTCHFIELD, R. S. and COVINGTON, M. W., Facilitation of Creative Thinking and Problem Solving in School Children. Paper presented at Symposium on Learning Research Pertinent to Educational Improvement, *Am. Ass. Adv. Sci.,* Cleveland, 1963.

DAVIES, G. B., Concrete and Formal Thinking Among Adolescent Children of Average Ability. Unpub. M.Ed. thesis, Birmingham University, 1964.

DE SILVA, W. A., Concept Formation in Adolescence History through Contextual Cues, with Special Reference to History Material. Unpub. Ph.D. thesis, School of Education, Birmingham University, 1969.

DUNCKER, K., On Problem Solving, *Psychol. Monogr.,* **58**, No. 5, A.P.A., Washington, 1945.

FLESCH, R., Measuring the Level of Abstraction, *J. Appl. Psychol.*, **34**, No. 6, pp. 384–90, 1950.

FREDERICKSEN, N., *Formulating Hypotheses*, Educ. Testing Service, Princeton, N.J., 1959.

GRAY, K., Programmed Cognitive Development, M.Ed. dissertation, School of Education, Birmingham University, 1970.

GUILFORD, J. P., The Structure of Intellect, *Psychol. Bull.*, **53**, pp. 267–93, 1956.

HERRICK, V. E. and TYLER, R., *Toward Improved Curriculum Theory*, Supp. Ed. Mon., University of Chicago Press, No. 71, 1950. See TYLER, R., The Organization of Learning Experiences, Chap. VI.

HILTON, M., Unpublished work on the effect of increased information on solving judgment problems, University of Birmingham, 1968.

HOTSON, LESLIE, *Mr W. H.*, Hart-Davis, London, 1964.

INHELDER, B. and PIAGET, J., *The Growth of Logical Thinking*, Routledge & Kegan Paul, London, 1958.

KORSTVEDT, A., STACEY, C. L., and REYNOLDS, W. F., Concept Formation of Normal and Subnormal Adolescents on a Modification of the Weigl-Goldstein-Scheerer Colour Form Sorting Test, *J. Clin. Psychol.* **10**, p. 88, 1954.

LAW, E. G., unpub. M.Ed. research on problem-solving in school mathematics, Birmingham University, 1968.

LAWTON, D., *Social Class, Language and Education*, Routledge & Kegan Paul, London, 1969.

LODWICK, A. R., Whether the Inference that Children Draw in Learning History Correspond to the Stages of Mental Development that Piaget Postulates. Unpub. dissertation, Dip. Ed., Birmingham University, 1958.

MARSTON, T. E., SHELTON, R. A. and PAINTER, G. D., *The Vinland Map and Tartar Relation*, Yale University Press, 1965.

MEALINGS, R. J., Some Aspects of Problem Solving in Science at the Secondary School State. Unpub. M.A. thesis, Birmingham University, 1961.

—— Problem Solving and Science Teaching, *Ed. Rev.*, **15**, pp. 194–207, 1963.

MILLER, F., *College Physics*, Harcourt & Brace, New York, 1959.

MILLETT, W. R., Logical Thinking in Maladjusted Boys. Dip. Child

Psy. research, School of Education, Birmingham University, 1967.

NOYES, H. P., The Physical Description of Elementary Particles, *Am. Scient.*, **45**, No. 5, December 1957.

PEEL, E. A., The Measurement of Interests by Verbal Methods, *Br. J. Statist. Psychol.*, **XII**, 11, p. 105, November 1958.

—— Experimental Examination of Some of Piaget's Schemata, *Br. J. Educ. Psychol.*, **29**, Pt. 2, p. 89, 1959.

—— Curiosity and Interest in Motivating School Learning. Proc. XIV Int. Congress Appl. Psychol., pp. 153–60, Copenhagen, 1961.

—— *The Pupil's Thinking*, Oldbourne, London, 1962.

—— pp. 122–5, Second Edition, 1968.

—— Intellectual Growth During Adolescence, *Educ. Rev.*, **17**, 3, pp. 169–80, June 1965.

—— A Study of Differences in the Judgments of Adolescent Pupils, *Br. J. Educ. Psychol.*, **XXXVI**, pp. 77–86, February 1966.

—— I, Historical Ideas and Concepts; II, The Pupils' Thinking and Inference, in BURSTON, W. H. and THOMSON, D. (eds.), *Studies in the Nature and Teaching of History*, Routledge & Kegan Paul, London, 1967.

—— A Method for Investigating Children's Understanding of Certain Logical Connectives Used in Binary Propositional Thinking, *Br. J. Math. & Stat. Psychol.*, **20**, Pt. 1, p. 81, May 1967.

—— Programmed Thinking, *Programmed Learning*, p. 155, July 1967.

—— Conceptual Learning and Explainer Thinking, in *Development in Learning* (eds.) LUNZER, E. A. and MORRIS, J. F., Vol. 2, Staples Press, London, 1968.

—— Generalizing and Abstracting, *Nature*, **230**, p. 600, April 1971.

PENROSE, L. S., Mechanics of Self Reproduction, *Ann. Hum. Genet.*, **23**, Pt. 1, pp. 59–72, 1958.

PERROTT, P. E., Unpublished research on adolescents' thinking in relation to field biology, Keele University, 1965.

PIAGET, J., *The Child's Construction of Reality*, Routledge & Kegan Paul, London, 1955.

—— Development and Learning, *J. Res. Sci. Teaching*, **2**, 1964.

RHYS, W. T., The Development of Logical Thought in the Adolescent with Reference to the Teaching of Geography in the Secondary School. Unpub. M.Ed. research, Birmingham University, 1964.

RUNCIMAN, W. C., *Social Sciences and Political Theory*, p. 12, Cambridge University Press, 1963.

SANDERSON, R. T., Principles of Chemical Reaction, *J. of Chem. Educ.*, **41**, No. 1, pp. 13–22, January 1964.

SCHLESINGER, A. M., *The Birth of the Nation*, Hamish Hamilton, London, 1969.

SCHOOLS COUNCIL WORKING PAPER, No. 2, Raising the School Leaving Age, 1965.

SMOKE, K. L., An Objective Study of Concept Formation, *Psychol. Monogr.*, **XLII**, No. 4, (Whole No. 191), 1932.

STANLEY, E., *Education and the Structure of Knowledge*, Rand McNally, Chicago, 1965.

STONES, S. K., An Analysis of the Growth of Adolescent Thinking in Relation to Their Comprehension of School History Material. Dip. Child Psy. research, School of Education, Birmingham University, 1965.

—— Factors Influencing the Capacity of Adolescents to Think in Abstract Terms in the Understanding of History. M.Ed. research, Manchester University, 1967.

SUCHMAN, J. R., Inquiry Training: Building Skills for Autonomous Discovery, *Merrill-Palmer Quart. Behav. & Dev.*, **7**, 3, pp. 147–69, 1961.

—— The Illinois Studies in Inquiry Training, *J. of Res. in Sci. Teaching*, **2**, pp. 230–32, 1964.

Sunday Times, Is the Vinland Map a Forgery? London, 6 March 1966.

TATON, R., *Reason and Chance in Scientific Discovery*, pp. 127–8, transl. A. J. POMERANS, Sci. Editions, New York, 1962.

THOMAS, D. I., Children's Understanding of Archaeological Material. Unpub. research, Dept. of Education, Birmingham University, 1966, reported by PEEL in BURSTON, W. H. and THOMSON, D., (eds.), *Studies in the Nature and Teaching of History*, Routledge & Kegan Paul, London, 1967.

VALENTINE, C. W., *Reasoning Tests for Higher Levels of Intelligence*, Oliver and Boyd, Edinburgh, 1954.

WASON, P. C., On the Failure of Eliminate Hypotheses in a Conceptual Task, *Quart. J. Expl. Psychol.*, **12**, 129, 1960.

WELLS, J., unpub. research on secondary school pupils' explanation of science problems. School of Education, Birmingham University, 1970.

WERNER, H. and KAPLAN, E., The Acquisition of Word Meanings: a Developmental Study, Monog. *Social Res. Child Dev.*, **15**, No. 1 (Whole No. 151), 1950.

WHELLOCK, R. B., A Test of Thinking in Terms of Science, unpub. thesis, M.A. Educ., London University, 1952.

WOOD, D. M., Some Concepts of Social Relations in Childhood and Adolescence. M.Ed. thesis, Nottingham University, 1964.

INDEX